THE SEVEN FACES
OF PHILANTHROPY

Russ Alan Prince
Karen Maru File

THE SEVEN FACES
OF PHILANTHROPY

A New Approach to
Cultivating Major Donors

JOSSEY-BASS
A Wiley Company
www.josseybass.com

Published by

JOSSEY-BASS
A Wiley Company
989 Market Street
San Francisco, CA 94103-1741

www.josseybass.com

Jossey-Bass books and products are available through most bookstores. To contact Jossey-Bass directly, call (888) 378-2537, fax to (800) 605-2665, or visit our website at www.josseybass.com.

Substantial discounts on bulk quantities of Jossey-Bass books are available to corporations, professional associations, and other organizations. For details and discount information, contact the special sales department at Jossey-Bass.

We at Jossey-Bass strive to use the most environmentally sensitive paper stocks available to us. Our publications are printed on acid-free recycled stock whenever possible, and our paper always meets or exceeds minimum GPO and EPA requirements.

Library of Congress Cataloging-in-Publication Data

Prince, Russ Alan, date.
 The seven faces of philanthropy : a new approach to cultivating major donors/Russ Alan Prince, Karen Maru File. — 1st ed.
  p. cm.—(The Jossey-Bass nonprofit and public management series)
 Includes bibliographical references and index.
 ISBN 0-7879-0008-7 (hardback)
 ISBN 0-7879-6057-8 (paperback)
 1. Fund raising—United States. 2. Philanthropists—United States. I. File, Karen.
II. Title. III. Series.
HV41.9.U5P74 1994
361.7'068'1—dc20   94-8095

FIRST EDITION
HB Printing   10 9 8 7 6
PB Printing   10 9 8 7 6 5 4 3 2 1

Contents

Preface

Cultivating major donors can be rewarding, gratifying, and even fun. It can also be an arduous and frustrating process. The best development officers are always on the lookout for insights, frameworks, and tools to help them become more effective and efficient in building mutually beneficial relationships with affluent individual donors. *The Seven Faces of Philanthropy* provides a new framework for fund raising and development.

The Seven Faces Framework

What sets the Seven Faces framework apart from other systems is that it is donor-centered. It involves a detailed understanding of the concerns, interests, needs, and motivations of affluent individual donors as they think about philanthropy. By categorizing wealthy donors into seven motivational types, development officers and nonprofit executives gain new perspectives for understanding and cultivating their donor base. For example, *communitarians* are defined as business owners motivated to improve the quality of life in their own communities and to reinforce their personal networks. They often become major donors to local, community-oriented nonprofits.

Another group of donors, called *Investors,* has general interest in philanthropy but specific interest in managing their personal financial portfolios (often assets derived from private business ownership) and in taking full advantage of the various tax and estate-planning benefits of charitable contributions. Each of the other five Faces — *Repayers, the Devout, Altruists, Dynasts,* and *Socialites* — has its own distinctive profile.

When a nonprofit determines which philanthropic personalities are concentrated in its affluent individual donor population, it can create more appropriate and effective development strategies. Clearly, working one-on-one with donors can be more effective when a fund raiser clearly understands the donor's motivations, and the Seven Faces framework provides such insights. Donor development programs can also be tailored to specific profiles. For example, an East Coast community foundation discovered that Communitarians and Investors were significant donor groups for them. Since both philanthropic personalities are characterized by a high incidence of private business ownership, the community foundation teamed up with a national accounting firm to provide seminars on how owners of family businesses can use closely held stock or options in charitable giving. The result: thirty-six business owners (44.4 percent of the seminar participants) ultimately donated in this manner and increased contributions 15 percent over the previous year.

Background and Approach

Our motivations for undertaking the research that led to writing this book were simple. Since we were both trained in the social sciences, we were aware of many instances in which developing a typology, or framework, to describe types of human behavior has been useful in moving a field forward. Because our careers have focused on working with nonprofits in various capacities, we saw an opportunity to advance the field by developing a framework of donor behavior. Thus, the Seven Faces framework, built on a multiyear program of research and testing, is an application of social science methods to the development field.

Overview of the Contents

The Introduction provides an extensive description of the social science and research methods used to create the framework. It details the process for interviewing donors and obtaining quotations to enliven the data, and gives a brief overview of the Seven Faces themselves.

Part One of the book, Chapters One through Seven, is made up of separate chapters on each of the seven philanthropic personalities. The purpose is to provide the reader with as clear a sense of each type as possible. Each is profiled demographically and motivationally. The chapters describe what each type looks for in a successful nonprofit relationship, their view of giving, and their perception of other donors. Our intention is to be sufficiently detailed that a reader will begin to identify donors they know in terms of these types—"Mrs. Smith is a Repayer because of her cancer," or "I see, Alan really fits the Altruist type; that's why he doesn't really want recognition," or "Mr. Douglas keeps asking all those questions about costs because he is an Investor."

Part Two details a four-step model to help development officers cultivate affluent donors by applying the Seven Faces framework. The first step, in Chapter Eight, outlines a process for making connections through charity networks that enables nonprofit executives to meet and identify new donors. Of course donors, like people generally, are more complex than one type; but donors, like all humans, have attitude and behavior patterns that do form a constellation of effects. Thus, identifying what overall type best describes a donor will help a fund raiser predict other aspects of that donor's behavior—such as their extent of involving outside advisors, their degree of networking with other donors, their desire for public recognition, and their preferences for involvement with the nonprofit. The chapter also provides ways fund raisers can leverage the charity networks donors participate in to broaden the base of support.

In Chapter Nine, step two provides a set of ideas development officers can use to position their nonprofit effectively with donors of a particular type. These ideas include

specific language found to be especially effective in discussing the nonprofit's goals and mission as well as in making case
statements particularly relevant to each type of donor.

Step three, in Chapter Ten, shows how the different
philanthropic personalities have differing levels of awareness,
knowledge, and interest in the various giving strategies available to them and the nonprofit. For example, fund raisers
should know of the surge of interest in foundations. They
should be aware that Dynasts are the best informed and know
which philanthropic personalities are most interested in
trusts. This chapter also demonstrates that a significant opportunity for educating donors about giving options is open
to nonprofits, since many donors want to know more about
these complex, but important, alternatives.

The final step in the individual donor cultivation process is provided in Chapter Eleven. This chapter documents
many ways a nonprofit can increase donor involvement in
a manner appropriate to each of the Seven Faces and build
long-term relationships.

These four steps, and the insights provided in the chapters detailing the Seven Faces, can be used in the context
of capital campaigns, major gift solicitation, and planned giving programs. The Seven Faces framework is designed to supplement, not replace, strategies and techniques that expert
fund raisers already use.

June 1994   Russ Alan Prince
                                               Stratford, Connecticut

                                               Karen Maru File
                                               Fairfield, Connecticut

The Authors

Russ Alan Prince is president of Prince & Associates, a leading consultancy in the private wealth field. Prince & Associates works with nonprofits, private banks, insurance companies, and investment management firms on strategic issues involving the private wealth markets.

In demand as a speaker on philanthropic topics, Prince has been cited as an expert in the area by the *New York Times*, the *Wall Street Journal*, *Fortune*, *Forbes*, and the *Washington Post*.

A prolific writer, Prince is a columnist for leading financial industry magazines and author of fifteen books, several coauthored with Karen File. His current new project is a Web-based interview series with leaders in the convergence of the nonprofit and financial services sectors.

Prince received his B.A. degree (1979) in liberal arts and his M.A. degree (1985) in sociology from the State University of New York at Stonybrook, where he was elected to Phi Beta Kappa and was a Lehman Fellow. He received his M.B.A. degree (1987) from the Columbia University Graduate School of Business, where he was a Dean's Scholar.

Karen Maru File is associate professor of marketing at the University of Connecticut at Stamford and teaches in the MBA program. She is author of several dozen academic articles. Her long-term research interests include global wealth, professional services marketing, and philanthropy, interests that led to her collaboration with Russ Alan Prince and Prince & Associates. She and Prince frequently coauthor books. Currently, she is exploring the impact of equity market changes on wealth attitudes and behavior.

Before taking up a university post, File was vice president and partner at Booz Allen & Hamilton in the marketing research consulting division. In that role, she led case assignments undertaken for nonprofits, among them the Boy Scouts of America, AARP (formerly known as the American Association of Retired Persons), the American Cancer Society, and Harvard University. She also developed a specialization in cause-related marketing that involves joint ventures between commercial firms and nonprofits.

File received her B.A. degree (1969) in government from Cornell University, her M.A. degree (1972) in urban affairs from Boston University, and her Ph.D. degree (1979) in sociology from Temple University. She has been selected for inclusion in *Who's Who in American Women* and Beta Gamma Sigma, the marketing honorary society. In her previous appointment at the University of Bridgeport, she was named to the Henry W. Littlefield Professorship.

Introduction to the Paperback Edition

When we wrote *The Seven Faces of Philanthropy* in 1993, we called our approach a new philosophy. At that time, it was a new idea to concentrate on the donor, to see the charitable process from the donor's point of view, and to cultivate relationships with donors on that basis. Now, at the time of writing the introduction to this paperback edition of the book, donor-centered fund raising is well established. The Seven Faces approach is more applicable than ever before, but it is no longer new.

Many of the important ideas first set out in *The Seven Faces of Philanthropy* are still true. First and foremost, donor motivation counts. The greatest case statement in the world is useless unless it matches up with the motivations of at least some donors. Donors are stakeholders in charitable institutions, and their voice is as important as those of constituents and staff. Donors want a role in institution building, and it is up to charitable institutions as well as professional development officers to help them find a way to participate meaningfully.

Another major idea in *The Seven Faces of Philanthropy* is that donors have an actual philanthropic career—that is, a career with a nonprofit. They start out small and grow into major donors only after long and careful development of a relationship. The relationship has to be as gratifying emotionally to the major donor as it is financially gratifying to the institution. This idea doesn't sound shocking today, but it was in 1993.

Then there is the big idea that in their relationships with nonprofits, different kinds of donors vary in the ways they want to be involved. Among the seven types (faces) described in this book, there are those (Socialites) who want to throw the benefit balls, those (Investors) who want to join the financial committee of the board, and those (Repayers) who want to know the details of constituent programs. The task of development professionals is to identify precisely how donors want to be involved and to make that happen. This is another idea that sounds commonplace today because the field has come a long way in a short period of time.

Yet another idea is that donors want to give their money in different ways. In the case of a big gift, a major donor will receive considerable advice from legal and tax experts as to how the gift should be structured, and structuring can vary. The development professional needs to know how to support this process and work effectively with all the professional advisors who get involved. Again, this is now standard operating procedure, and many significant gifts have resulted from this expansion of the development professional's role.

Still another big idea is that it is important to talk to donors about topics that are meaningful to them and in ways that are effective with them. Not all donors want to know the same things about an institution. Donors, like the rest of us, tune out if talked to in ways they find irrelevant or boring. One of our favorite portions of the *Seven Faces* book is the table showing how the different donor personality types responded to certain key words. That small study validated our proposition that the one-size-fits-all case statement can never be as effective as tailored and customized communications.

Whereas it is nice to have been right, it is even nicer to be joined by many other researchers who are also adding their own rich findings. It is gratifying to us that there are now many different ways to think about donor-centeredness. We have always argued that the Seven Faces is but a tool in a development officer's toolkit, and that there is much room for complementary approaches. Since the time *The Seven Faces of Philanthropy* was written, many new streams of research into donor motivations have emerged, resulting in a more responsive donor-centeredness. There is provocative and useful research into the role of gender in philanthropy, research that helps development professionals talk, interact, and work more effectively with men and with women. There is very significant research into philanthropic traditions in different cultures, research with important implications for institutions with Latino, Asian-American, African-American, and other populations in their prospective donor bases. Because of all the new research findings available, development officers can select the approaches that are most meaningful to them and to the institutions they represent.

This means development professionals are newly empowered throughout the entire development process. By dynamically selecting among all the tools available to them, they can craft "situational strategies" for creating stewardship that is meaningful for both donor and institution. By tailoring their approach to a specific donor profile that takes into account such donor traits as philanthropic personality, gender, cultural tradition, and philanthropic life cycle, development professionals can respond in a way that is gratifying for the donor, comfortable for the development officer, and effective for the institution.

At its core, the chief benefit of the Seven Faces approach is the process. If those responsible for institutional advancement discipline themselves to ask, Which face is this donor? What would motivate him or her to support my organization? What would he or she want from a charitable relationship with my cause? they begin the process of donor-centered relationship development.

In the years since the book was written, it has become established that donor-centered fund raising is the state-of-the-art. Donor-centered fundraising is more efficient than traditional kinds of fund raising: development officers spend their time on better prospects. It is more effective: larger sums are raised. It is also more profitable (in a charitable as well as a business sense): donors cultivated in this way, over the span of their charitable career, give larger amounts to the nonprofit.

In retrospect, the Seven Faces concept of donor-centered development found easy acceptance because it was an idea whose time had truly come. It superseded a highly necessary phase of thinking about cause and mission. Nonprofits had to clarify mission and purpose before they could effectively enlist donors in their cause. With the Seven Faces and subsequent tools for donor-centered development available to them, nonprofits were able to achieve new levels of resources available for programs.

We are often asked, What's next? What is the next big idea in fund raising? In our view, the circle is now complete. Nonprofits know their mission and their resource development praxis. Best of all, fund raising has become a true profession. The best development officers we know use all the tools and use them well. "What's next" in development is likely to be cycles of refinement and improvement rather than one big idea or the next new thing. All the building blocks to success are now in place; it is up to development professionals to use them well.

We do know that some things will not strongly affect major gifts. Although much is said about technology (read: the Internet) we know that technology will not significantly affect the development process with philanthropists and major donors. Sure, technology can and will support the institutional advancement process. Web-based programs exist to augment or replace costly direct mail campaigns for smaller donors. In many major donor management software systems we have seen, there are now ways to tag or label donors based on their segment or personality or motivational or psychographic characteristics. This sort of tagging is helpful to the development professional with many donors in the major gift process. But does anyone in the field imagine that it will ever be possible to replace the major gifts development professional with a Web site? No. Institutions need a human face and that face is the development officer. There is too much subtlety and complexity to the strategic situation of working with a prospective major donor. No, the major gifts development professional is here to stay and even grow in importance.

We are grateful to all the people who recognized our work and ran with it. There is nothing more gratifying to researchers and authors than to truly have an impact in their field.

September 2001   Russ Alan Prince
Karen Maru File
Shelton, Connecticut

To Sandi Jean Bower Prince
  for making every day a special treat
and to Zita Prince
  for teaching me to care even when I wasn't interested
        —Russ Alan Prince

To Joe, Charlie, and Mike
        —Karen Maru File

Introduction:
A Powerful New Tool for
Understanding Major Donors

During the 1990s, already profound stressors on the nonprofit sector will become even stronger. To meet social needs, the number of nonprofit causes are multiplying (Ben-Ner and Van Hoomissen, 1990) while the resources required to achieve their objectives are not increasing at the same rate (McMurtry, Netting, and Kettner, 1991). The financial needs of the nonprofit sector are outpacing resource development, resulting in a need to create ever more efficient resource development programs, particularly programs designed to cultivate affluent individual donors.

As environmental stressors increase on the third sector, success will be achieved through introducing new approaches for resource development. Over the years, fund raising has consistently innovated methods for nonprofit resource development (Seymour, 1966). One of the most promising for affluent donor development, donor segmentation, is the topic of this book. Donor segmentation is the process of classifying the presently undifferentiated group of wealthy individual donors into a small number of groups based on similarities in their views about philanthropy. Donor segmentation allows nonprofit organizations to determine which affluent individual donor segments offer the best potential for long-term and major gift support, and enables these organizations to tailor communications such as case statements selected segments' needs. As a result, donor segmentation enables a nonprofit to use resources most efficiently. The donor segmentation approach offers four principal advantages to nonprofit resource development managers as they target major donors (Johnson, 1986; Leibtag, 1986; Wills, 1985):

1. *Efficient identification* of current and prospective donor groups
2. *Clear selection criteria* for developing these benefactors efficiently (Cermak, File, and Prince, 1991)
3. *Ability to tailor* solicitation methods appropriately
4. *Basis for the design* of ongoing relationship-management programs geared to donors' needs (Prince, 1991)

The four-year research program undertaken for this book has resulted in the identification of seven distinctive segments of affluent individual donors. Each segment is one of the Seven Faces of Philanthropy.

Donor segmentation stems from the considerable body of research on philanthropy. The first section of this chapter describes what has already been discovered about affluent donor motivations, traces insights from prior work as well as gaps in knowledge, and suggests the value of donor segmentation. The second section shows that the gap in knowledge about the motivations of the affluent can be addressed through the approach to donor segmentation used here: benefit segmentation. This section also traces the history of benefit segmentation and describes the research program undertaken to apply benefit segmentation to the third sector.

Previous Studies of Major Donors

A number of studies have explored the charitable motivations and practices of small donors such as those who contribute to United Way campaigns (Harvey, 1990; Guy and Patton, 1988; Smith, 1980) and analyzed philanthropic patterns over time in the U.S. economy (Weisbrod, 1988; Jencks, 1987). Because of the relative importance of affluent individual donors, their needs, motivations, and strategies have been the focus of many studies during the past decade. These studies are the foundation for the donor segmentation approach of the Seven Faces research program (Magat, 1990; Prince, 1993).

Panus on Motivations for Major Gifts

The number of philanthropists who give more than a million dollars in any given year is small, but Panus (1984) interviewed twenty such individual donors in depth. A major result of his research was the identification of twenty-two motivations that one or more of the philanthropists expressed for making a major gift. These motivations included such factors as "community responsibility and civic pride," "tax considerations," and "religious or spiritual affiliation of the institution." Panus, a consultant to nonprofits and their financial resource development personnel, documented many of the themes extended by the Seven Faces donor segmentation research program.

The importance of exploring motives from the donor perspective is emphasized by another portion of the Panus study. In a series of follow-up surveys, nonprofits were asked to rate how important they thought each of the twenty-two motivations was to philanthropists. Consistent, significant differences were found between what donors said motivated them and what nonprofits thought motivated donors. For example, donors rated the fiscal stability of the nonprofit 7.4 on a 10-point scale, while nonprofits estimated donors would rate it much lower (4.7). For this and other reasons, the Seven Faces research program is thoroughly grounded in donor self-descriptions of their motivations and interests.

Boris on Motivations for Creating Foundations

Foundations are one vehicle the affluent use to channel assets to nonprofits. Boris (1987) collected data on the motivations of donors establishing foundations; of the 435 respondents, 16 percent were donors themselves, the remainder were foundation staff providing data about donors. From these data, a factor analysis was used to reduce twenty reasons to six motivational dimensions: Altruism, Beliefs, Instrumental Motives, Memorial, Community, and Peer Pressure. These motivational dimensions, in revised form, were included in the Seven Faces research program. Altruism and (religious) beliefs emerge as important for general giving among affluent individual donors as they are for establishing foundations. Instrumental motives, such as tax and estate considerations, concern many affluent donors. The desire to honor the memory of a loved one emerges in the Seven Faces work as well, but seems a situational rather than enduring motivation to give. Social pressures such as community ties and business and social peer groups also figure prominently in the Seven Faces research, as will be shown.

Odendahl on Charitable Motivations of Philanthropists

Odendahl (1990) used anthropological methods to discern patterns in philanthropic motivation among 140 wealthy donors. An emphasis on cultural factors, religious orientation, and lifestyle factors resulted in four philanthropic groupings: Dynasty and Philanthropy, Lady Bountiful, First Generation Man, and Elite Jewish Giving. This work showed the importance of distinguishing between philanthropists operating out of a multi-generation family tradition of giving inherited assets and those with first generation wealth who give personally earned assets for reasons unrelated to specific family values.

Odendahl's work also indicated the importance of religious motivations in giving. The historical and cultural relationships between religious orientation and philanthropy have received consistent attention in the literature on philanthropy (for a review see Wuthnow, Hodgkinson, and Associates, 1990). A contribution of Odendahl's work is that religious motivations vary across donors, being more relevant to some than to others. Gender and sex roles are also important. In

the Seven Faces research, the findings on religious motivations and dynastic family traditions were preserved in the
motivational set. Data on source of wealth (inherited or derived from a business), gender and sex role were collected
in another part of the questionnaire because they are not
motivations but characteristics of individual donors. This information was used to profile the various segments.

Schervish on Philanthropic Strategies

Rather than focus on a specific giving event, Schervish (1988;
1991) explored the long-term strategies donors choose in interacting with nonprofits. Lengthy, qualitative, and detailed
interviews with 130 millionaires explored aspects of values,
life experience, communication patterns, and interaction style
preferences with nonprofits. The conceptualization of philanthropy as a social relationship (Ostrander and Schervish, 1990)
was developed into a taxonomy of sixteen identifiable interaction patterns. These patterns are denoted as strategies,
which range from personal-engagement strategies (donors personally involved in delivering services to constituents) to
mediated-engagement strategies such as brokering (fund raising among other donors). In the Seven Faces work, donor
motivations (attitudes) were intentionally separated from behaviors (donating, recruiting, and volunteering) for theoreti-
cal and methodological reasons. However, the insight that
motivations and behaviors interact to create distinct segments
or groups of donors was preserved. The motivational items
alone were used to create the donor groups in the Seven
Faces research, but other portions of the questionnaire and
follow-up questionnaires explore in detail donor preferences
for ways of interacting with nonprofits.

Cermak, File, and Prince on Motivations for Planned Giving

A recent examination of the reasons donors establish charitable trusts provides an additional point of departure for the

Seven Faces study (Cermak, File, and Prince, 1991). In that study, a set of thirty-six benefit-oriented items were used to create segments based on the benefits donors sought in creating major trusts benefiting nonprofits. These items were drawn from the literature on philanthropy already discussed, as well as research on altruism, gift-giving, and prosocial behaviors. Cluster analysis of the items resulted in four donor segments: Affiliators, who look for social and business linkages through nonprofit-related activities; Pragmatists, who seek personal financial advantages through support of nonprofits; Dynasts, who are heirs to family affluence and to a tradition of philanthropy; and Repayers, who want to reciprocate benefits they or someone close to them received from a nonprofit. This segmentation scheme, like that of Boris and Odendahl, seemed, on reflection, to combine too many disparate motivations into a single segment. For example, it appeared as though enhancing business affiliations may be a different motive than enhancing social affiliations. The final Seven Faces study included a wider range of motivations and extended these frameworks.

Gaps in Previous Studies

A few themes emerge from this review of previous studies. One is that each of the various studies incorporated a somewhat different but often overlapping set of variables into their examination of donor motivations. The Seven Faces research program aimed to be comprehensive by including all the attitudinal and motivational variables identified by other researchers. The other observation is that data sets were rarely of sufficient size to permit quantitative analysis for this population. Previous research has either focused on less affluent donors (Harvey, 1990), with smaller numbers of donors leading to a form of qualitative analysis (Panus, 1984; Odendahl, 1990; Schervish, 1988), or with third parties reporting about major donors (Boris, 1987).

Thus, another objective of the Seven Faces research program was to create an unprecedented large data set of affluent individual donors so that quantitative forms of data analysis could be applied. In summary, the Seven Faces research is based on a comprehensive model, is empirically derived, provides more detail from a larger data set, is based on theory, and is development oriented.

Donor Segmentation

This section outlines the purposes and types of segmentation and describes the program of research for the Seven Faces study.

Segmentation: Purpose and Types

Nonprofit organizations already segment their donors in a number of ways depending on their objective (Kotler, 1991). For example, nonprofits find it useful to separate their donors into segments of small and large givers, a form of demographic segmentation which categorizes donors into groups based on characteristics such as income. Many nonprofits also use behavioral segmentation whenever sources of development are categorized by size of gift or potential for planned giving. Less widely used is psychographic segmentation which divides donors into groups or segments based on social class, lifestyle, or personality. The objective of segmentation, whatever form is elected, is to group donors who are similar in the way they give. If the segmentation process selected by a nonprofit is successful, development officers can tailor fund-raising strategies for the different needs of the various segments.

The segmentation approach with the most current relevance for nonprofits is the motivational segmentation approach. As defined by Kotler (1991), motivational, or benefit, segmentation "calls for identifying the major benefits that people look for . . . , [and] the kinds of people who look for each benefit" (p. 273). Motivational segmentation has been successfully used in many settings (Wills, 1990; Plummer, 1974; Wind, 1978).

It should be noted that motivational segmentation has

its critics. Two general groups of criticism are methodological and utilitarian. The methodological critiques caution that the statistics used in segmentation (typically factor and cluster analysis) are so powerful that segments will almost always be produced by these techniques if any underlying variance in the data is present. Care must be taken that any derived segments meet tests of reliability and validity, and procedures have been developed for these purposes. The appendix contains a discussion of what the current standards of reliability and validity are and how these standards have been met. The second general criticism of motivational segmentation is utilitarian; critics from this school point out that broad-based communications programs such as direct mail, telephone solicitation, or advertising cannot be used to reach motivational segments on a cost-efficient basis. This criticism does not pertain to the current application of motivational segmentation as affluent individual donor cultivation is a one-on-one process and mass communication approaches are not used for any purpose other than awareness-building.

The Program of Research Used Here

The relationship between donors and nonprofits can be considered one of social exchange. Donors enter a relationship with a nonprofit because they have certain motivations to do so. The systematic study of these motivations is possible through the formal structure of a segmentation study in which those motivations themselves become the basis for segmentation. To complete this motivationally based donor segmentation, a multi-year research program was undertaken. An overview of that research is presented here; additional details are provided in the appendix.

Phase I: Preliminary Segmentation Study. This quantitative study of 476 affluent individual donors explored planned giving and donor perspectives on the trust creation process in considerable detail. The study also explored the applicability and outcomes of motivational segmentation in a sample of major donors. The study resulted in the profiling of four motivational donor types, a result sufficiently promising to encourage the team to further extend the motivational segmentation approach. This study is in the process of being published (Cermak, File, and Prince, 1994).

Phase II: Intensive Testing of Motivational Items. Because the four segments appeared to combine donor types that might be better conceptualized separately, the research team decided to expand the number and breadth of motivational items. A new and more extensive questionnaire was designed. It contained the original motivational battery, more than forty new items drawn from the literature, over a dozen in-depth individual interviews with donors, and fifteen interviews with resource development personnel from a variety of nonprofits. This expanded questionnaire was administered to 123 affluent donors attending a weekend conference on charitable remainder trusts. Factor and cluster analysis of whole and split samples confirmed the split in the affiliation dimension between social and business affiliation benefits and revealed a new separation along a belief or values dimension that would distinguish those operating out of a religious paradigm from those prompted by an altruistic or self-development array of motives. On the basis of this intensive pretest, some motivational items were dropped and others reworded.

Phase III: Seven Faces Study. This final study forms the basis of the donor segmentation reported in this book (Prince, File, and Gillespie, 1993). For the purposes of this study, an affluent individual donor was defined as a person who maintains $1 million or more in a discretionary investment advisory account and who contributed $50,000 or more to a single nonprofit within the last two years. The individuals interviewed for the Seven Faces study are significantly more affluent than those usually comprising the top tier in surveys on giving; for example, a major national survey on giving had, as the top income category, all those who earned $100,000 and over and contributed an average of $2,329 (Hodgkinson, Weitzman, and the Gallup Organization, 1988). The sampling

design used to obtain this affluent group entailed networking through a number of professional service firms with an
affluent clientele. Ultimately, twelve professional service firms
from across the United States were enlisted to identify 218
donors meeting study criteria. Cluster analysis was selected
as the statistical approach of preference, and the seven-cluster
solution met the criteria set for this study, hence "Seven
Faces." The final cluster solution—the Seven Faces framework—was evaluated in focus groups of nonprofit resource
development managers and in focus groups of nonprofit executives who confirmed its validity in the context of their
own experience. To further validate the results, one of the
authors recontacted five or more members of each segment
and interviewed them at length over the telephone about
their motivations for giving. These follow-up interviews validated donors' segment membership in all cases.

Direct quotes of respondents from these and other
follow-up interviews are included in the various sections of
this book. These quotes were selected from hundreds of pages
of transcribed interviews to provide readers with direct access to donors' own expressions of their motivations and feelings. They are intended to provide fund raisers with another
way of relating to the material presented in the book. Experienced fund raisers should be able to use these quotes to
recognize their donors in the Seven Faces framework. These
quotes will also help less experienced fund raisers identify
and relate to donors more readily through their motivations.

Phase IV: Longitudinal and Special Focus Studies. The
Seven Faces approach is now in use at a number of nonprofits
across the United States. Under careful study conditions, as-
sessments to determine the framework's effectiveness for
resource development work are underway. A few examples
include:

- A *national professional association.* This association is interested in establishing a new foundation for the purpose
  of assisting association members. The Seven Faces ap-

proach was used to profile the membership in terms of their giving characteristics, to quantify the proportion most likely to support the foundation, and to select the most salient appeals the foundation could make toward the segments of the membership most likely to be supporters.

- *Regional medical centers.* The Seven Faces approach is being integrated into the current giving campaign of three centers, and an evaluation will be made of the incremental success that can be attributed to the use of the framework.
- *Public policy analysis.* Many of the initiatives suggested by the Clinton administration in Washington have implications for nonprofits and their affluent individual donors. The Seven Faces framework is being used as part of an ongoing panel study of affluent individual donor perceptions of public policies, especially tax reform.

Summary

The multiyear study culminating in the Seven Faces donor segmentation approach had its roots in previous studies of affluent individual donors. The over eight hundred individuals who participated at one stage or another of this study is the largest affluent population studied to date. The next section of the book profiles each of the seven donor types, including statistics and ample quotes from representative members. The final section of the book documents how fund raisers can incorporate the Seven Faces approach into strategy design for their own nonprofits.

Part One

PROFILING
THE SEVEN FACES OF
PHILANTHROPY

The research method used for this study places each affluent individual donor into one of seven distinct segments based on needs, motivations, and benefits the individual says are most important to him or her. The seven segments—the Seven Faces of Philanthropy—provide a framework for understanding major donors. (The relative proportions of each type are shown in Figure P.1.) Each segment represents a characteristic and distinctive way a donor group approaches philanthropy, a set of typical attitudes and beliefs, a range of considerations, a process of evaluation, and a style of involvement with nonprofits. Because these seven categories explain much of the range of major donor behavior, the Seven Faces framework can be useful to expand the perspectives fund raisers bring to their profession. The Seven Faces form of segmentation is revealing because one set of motivations tends to dominate people's decisions, even though close questioning will reveal that any individual donor will also feel additional motivations. Experienced fund raisers will recognize that the Seven Faces approach has limits and constraints. Motivational segmentation methodologies such as these simplify human motivations to some degree in order to provide a useful and easily applied framework. Like all such frame-

Figure P.1. The Seven Faces of Philanthropy.

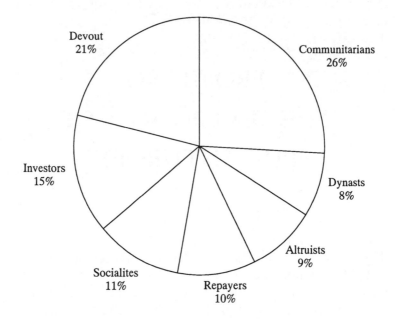

works or typologies, the Seven Faces is a tool best used in conjunction with the accumulated expertise of the fund raiser, not in place of it. Fund raisers have found the framework a useful heuristic to supplement their experience.

This part introduces the Seven Faces framework. The chapters that follow provide descriptions of each segment — the Seven Faces of philanthropy. Part Two presents a method of donor cultivation within the framework of relationship development and provides a method for identifying philanthropic personality, creating empathic relations, and validating the experience for the prospective donor in such a way as to build commitment.

The Communitarians: Doing Good Makes Sense

Communitarians, the largest segment (26.3%), give because it makes good sense to do so. Communitarians are typically local business owners who find that service on boards and committees of local nonprofits can be good for business because of the relationships that often develop in such settings. The other reason Communitarians believe active philanthropy makes good sense is that they help their own communities prosper by supporting local charities.

The Devout: Doing Good Is God's Will

The Devout are motivated to support nonprofits for religious reasons; they say they believe it is God's will for them to help others. Almost always members of a local church, which is part of a regional or national religious group, the Devout channel nearly all (96.4%) their giving to religious institutions. The Devout make up the second largest group (20.9%) of major donors.

The Investor: Doing Good Is Good Business

Investors are affluent individual donors who give with one eye on the nonprofit cause and one eye on personal tax and estate consequences. Investors calibrate their giving to take advantage of tax and estate benefits and therefore want to work with nonprofits that understand these concerns. To achieve their tax, estate, and philanthropic interests, Investors donate to a wide range of nonprofits and are the segment most likely to support umbrella nonprofits such as community foundations (22.5%). About 15.3 percent of major donors are Investors.

The Socialite: Doing Good Is Fun

Socialites find social functions benefiting nonprofits an especially appealing way to help make a better world and have a good time doing it. Socialites are members of local social networks with which they interact to select nonprofits for support and to leverage in fund-raising activities. They seek opportunities to create fund raisers and social events benefiting nonprofits, and are less interested in participating in the day-to-day operations of the nonprofit or activities directed at constituents. Socialites, who tend to support the arts and education as well as religious nonprofits, make up 10.8 percent of major donors.

The Altruist: Doing Good Feels Right

Altruists embody the popular perception of the selfless donor—the donor who gives out of generosity and empathy to urgent causes and who modestly "wishes to remain anonymous." Altruists give because they believe it is a moral imperative, and because it helps them grow as human beings or evolve spiritually. Altruists make giving decisions without the input of advisors and are not usually interested in active roles in the nonprofits they support. A far greater proportion of Altruists than any other group focus their philanthropy on social causes. Nine percent of major donors are Altruists.

The Repayer: Doing Good in Return

Repayers tend to have been constituents first and donors second. A typical Repayer has personally benefited from some institution, often a school or medical center, and now supports that institution from a feeling of loyalty or obligation. Repayers concentrate their philanthropy on medical charities and educational institutions. Repayers are 10.2 percent of major donors.

The Dynast: Doing Good Is a Family Tradition

Unlike other segments, Dynasts typically inherit their wealth. The philanthropic motivation of Dynasts stems from their socialization. Giving is something their family has always stood for and they believe it is expected of them to support nonprofits. However, younger Dynasts will seek out different philanthropies than their parents. Although Dynasts have been significant figures in philanthropy for some time, they now comprise 8.3 percent of major donors.

1

The Communitarian:
Doing Good Makes Sense

If I'm going to help someone, it's sure going to be my neighbors.
We've got to stick together and make life for everyone here in
the community just a little bit better.

This country was built on each and every man, woman, and child
pitching in to help. This is the value that makes our communities and our nation strong. This is the value that I have, to help
my neighbors and my community. I help charities that help them
and that way I'm helping the country. It's the best way to make
charity mean something special.

Who Are the Communitarians?

Fund raisers often instinctively recognize Communitarians.
If there is such a thing as a typical group of major donors,
Communitarians are it. Communitarians are the largest philanthropic segment, including 26.3 percent of all major donors.
Most (75.6%) are owners of home-town businesses and most
(91.1%) are male. Because typical Communitarians founded
their businesses after World War II, their formal education
is lower on the average (for 55.4%, the highest educational
level is high school). Because Communitarians believe their

17

fortune is intertwined with that of their community, their philanthropy is directed toward community needs. For Communitarians, doing good works in and for the place they live only makes sense.

Why Communitarians Give

Communitarians give because they want to give something back to their communities for all the advantages they themselves have received. This sense of obligation to give back links Communitarians to Repayers, but their unwavering focus on their communities sets them apart. Communitarians think of themselves as fair and equitable, they deeply feel the advantages provided by their communities, and they desire to improve the quality of life in those communities even further.

Communitarians are sharp and successful business people. They know that many business connections are established by people sitting around charity boardroom tables, and they want to reserve their seats. However, while Communitarians are well aware of the business benefits of philanthropic involvement, their primary motivation is desire to better their communities.

Communitarians are affluent enough to do good works and think their depth of experience in local affairs makes them quite capable of doing so effectively. They believe private philanthropy is a choice, not an obligation, and they feel that local nonprofits are better suited than government initiatives to solve social problems.

Communitarians Give Because Nonprofits Are More Effective Than Government Programs

Almost all Communitarians (92.9%) believe strongly that nonprofits are more effective in addressing social and human problems than are federal, state, and local governments. Most philanthropists would generally agree, but Communitarians stand out for their skepticism of government-sponsored programs.

I help elect some of those politicians. They might be nice people but when they get in office they seem to lose sight of what's
important. I think it is the people in the neighborhoods, people
like me, who work with charity organizations that care, that meet
the needs of society. Not politicians. Not government.

I can guarantee you that politicians can't do half the job as the
nonprofits that are here in the county. Not when it comes to
helping people.

Communitarians believe that governments, even state
governments, are too far removed from local concerns to be
effective. Communitarians agree that it is local leaders, business leaders like themselves, who know the problems on a
day-to-day basis and who are best at designing solutions
through nonprofits. In their view, the job of creating positive social change should be the responsibility of local leaders
highly involved with local nonprofits.

The only way to make a difference is to get your hands dirty.
Crying to the state house isn't going to do anything for anyone.
You have to become involved to get anything done, and that
means charity work.

Communitarians Believe Wealthy Donors Give
Because They Want to, Not out of a Sense of Obligation

Few Communitarians (10.7%) believe that they, or other
wealthy people, are morally obligated to give. Instead, they
(along with Investors and Socialites) view giving to nonprofits
as a voluntary, discretionary act.

Some people say, it's a wealthy person's moral responsibility to
help those who are less fortunate. If you are successful, you have
to give back to society. Let's get real; no one has to be philanthropic. I am because I want to be, and I suspect that it's the
same for everyone else.

Wealth doesn't equate to philanthropy any more than it equates to stinginess or sincerity or anything at all. Wealth means money pure and simple. I think it's plain foolish to think that having money makes a person have to do anything but pay more taxes. The philanthropy is because a person wants to, never because they have to.

Communitarians share a sense of having made their wealth on their own as business owners. They made it "the hard way," without "handouts," and others should too. If they choose to put a little back into the community, that's fine, but no one should take it for granted.

I sacrificed to get where I am. I don't owe anyone a thing. I give because it suits me to give, and that has nothing to do with any moral feeling.

Rich or poor doesn't make a damn bit of difference. This has nothing to do with class issues or such nonsense. Being wealthy doesn't make it that I've got to support worthy causes any more than being poor means I've got to volunteer. We're charitable because we want to be and that's it.

Communitarians Give Because It Is Good Sense to Support Your Local Community

Many Communitarians have deep roots in their communities and operate out of a sense of linkage to the history of the place. The majority of Communitarians (85.2%) agree that those with wealth should support their local community.

My family has lived in this town for more than two generations and I'm not about to move. I choose to give to charities in my community, because that's where my roots are.

This community is my home, my family's home. It's part of my life. For me, it lives, it breathes. I want to do everything I can to make it that way for my kids and, hopefully, their kids. That's why I concentrate all my charity on keeping the breath of life strong in the place.

At the same time, Communitarians see themselves in a web of interlocking relationships in their local communities. Their businesses often buy supplies locally and sell goods and services locally. They tend to hire locally, obtain finance locally, and invest locally. Because they have been successful, Communitarians recognize a strong psychological bond to their local environment, a bond they are intent in reinforcing. Further cementing local relationships with philanthropic activities makes good business sense as well as good personal sense. Since most (75.6%) are successful business owners, Communitarians are quick to recognize that helping their community also reinforces business ties.

In this area, all the business leaders are involved with the symphony. Frankly, a whole lot of business deals get made at symphony board meetings.

Everybody important is around at charity board meetings and you get to talking. I'd be a fool and out of business if I didn't join a lot of boards and take that opportunity to make a business deal every chance I got.

Communitarians mainly support local cultural, religious, and educational concerns (79.2% of their donations go to such causes), and they select nonprofits oriented to serving the needs of their community.

I will only give to good causes that help out the town. I have to let other people be concerned about what's happening in other parts of the world.

I was born here, I married a local girl, I raised my kids here, and I will die here. This is where my philanthropy goes and it always will. I have never considered giving money to a charity that wasn't located here.

Communitarians Give Because It Is
in Their Self Interest to Do So

Most Communitarians (78.6%) agree that it is completely acceptable for philanthropy to be as good for the giver as it is for the recipient. Communitarians view philanthropy as exchange, just like their businesses are. The way they see it, they provide financial and personal support to nonprofits and in return receive the positive feelings associated with being philanthropic, and some business connections as well. This is a different perspective than the traditional view that philanthropic support is altruistic or selfless in nature. While some donor segments do think of philanthropy as altruistic or selfless (see especially the Altruists and the Devout in later sections), Communitarians believe that relationships with nonprofits, just like relationships in business, can be win-win. This view of philanthropy as exchange is shared by several other philanthropic personalities.

> I don't see any reason you shouldn't get something out of giving. If I give, people who need it get help, the nonprofit gets help, and I get a little boost too. So why not?

> I'm a businessman. And as a businessman I know what's important in business and that's making a buck. It's the same for the charities. I don't see a single thing wrong with giving a little to get a little.

How Communitarians Select Nonprofits

Communitarians have an overriding preference for local causes and local operations. If a nonprofit they support is a national organization, they prefer to support the local chapter.

> I'm a big supporter of the United Way. When I think of the United Way, I'm not thinking about the national organization, I'm thinking about the local chapter. For me, that's what the United Way is.

> If it isn't going to my neighbors, I don't see any reason to give
> my money to a charitable organization. The money in this
> town should stay in the town, not go off somewhere else.

Communitarians are business people, and this orientation permeates their attitudes and behaviors. When Communitarians evaluate nonprofits, they look for evidence of businesslike characteristics such as solid management practices and a proven track record of results. They seek the same qualities in a nonprofit that they associate with a successful business. Communitarians research candidate nonprofits carefully and are likely to rely on advisors as well.

In Selecting Nonprofits, Communitarians Look for Effectiveness

Almost all Communitarians (91.9%) take their responsibility to evaluate nonprofits seriously. Communitarians feel that giving should follow a period of data collection, personal experience, advice of other businesspeople, and analysis of alternative nonprofits. Communitarians look for solid evidence of well managed business operations and a record of results. They do not generally accept promises or good intentions. Communitarians are concerned with achievements and therefore tend not to be moved by plans for the future. At the same time, Communitarians, because of their extensive involvement in local affairs, believe they are uniquely well equipped to judge the effectiveness of local nonprofits.

> People working in a nonprofit may have good intentions, but
> good intentions aren't enough. Getting the job done is what's
> important. I find and give my money to groups that can make
> a real difference. I live here; I can see what's going on.
>
> I'm not into throwing my money away. So, I give to charities
> that do a good job. Because I give to charities I live with, I'm
> always able to tell if they are using the money well.

Communitarians Use Advisors
Extensively in Making Donation Decisions

About half of Communitarians (51.4%) regularly use a professional to formally advise them on their charitable contributions. These philanthropic advisors are of two general types. One is the financial/legal advisor who, over the years, has become a friend. This individual provides such advice as part of the ongoing personal and professional relationship.

> Jack, my lawer, has been with me from the beginning. He knows me well. Sometimes, better than my wife. To make the giving I do have meaning and accomplish what I think it should, I go to Jack to help me get results. It's the logical thing to do, and besides, he knows everybody in the community.

> I've been with the bank since I started my firm — I trust them. They do business with everybody in town and they have a keen feeling of who is doing good work. I'm just piggybacking on people who know the place.

Aside from the fact that these financial/legal advisors are personally close to the Communitarian and are usually well connected in the community, their professional expertise comes into play. That is, they provide counsel on the best way to give so that the Communitarian's personal financial agenda is met along with the philanthropic one.

> You can give smart or give foolish, and I'd rather give smart. My accountant makes sure I get the most for my charity and that also means the best deal with Uncle Sam.

> When I give, I need to make sure it's a fiscally wise thing to do and that when I do it, it's done with all the tax advantages lined up. That means turning to professionals; that's what I pay them for.

Some Communitarians will turn to trusted people other than attorneys or bankers for advice. For instance, one Communitarian who uses the services of a priest, said:

Father is so hooked into what's going on around here and he's so into doing the right thing, he's the best source of information you can imagine. While I give to the Church, Father also tells me about other charities and has helped me work things out.

Aside from these advisory networks, some Communitarians are turning to specialists in philanthropic advisory services. These individuals, who often come from the financial services/legal fields, concentrate on advising the wealthy in philanthropic matters and have established competence in the area. Other professional philanthropic advisors have entered this business from the world of fund raising and foundations. Their expertise concerning the nonprofit sector is what they offer. Some Communitarians have retained philanthropic advisors who are specialists in the field because it makes good sense to do so. The payoff is a qualified sounding board for their philanthropic decisions.

The tax, business, social and charitable aspects of giving are just getting too complicated. There are professional people out there who know lots more about these charities than I do. Why not use them? In my experience, I found they're worth the cost.

To make a splash, a really big splash, you have to know a lot about what you're doing. It doesn't matter if it's running a business or giving to charity. For my business, I hire consultants all the time to be more effective. It only makes sense to do the same thing about giving to charity. I have lots of money riding on both types of decisions.

Some Communitarians do not employ philanthropic advisors because they are unaware there are such experts, but become interested when the concept is introduced to them. They readily recognize the many advantages of using experts in this area.

I made a good living by doing something people needed and no one else was doing. It figures that someone would get the idea of helping people to do a good job of being charitable. If I knew someone who did it, I'd be willing to hire them to help me out.

But most simply feel they know enough about their communities to make the decisions. Their extensive personal involvement in the community is more than sufficient to enable them to comfortably make philanthropic decisions.

What Communitarians Look for After the Gift

Some Communitarians would frankly like to have some control over the uses of their donated funds. They would like to help direct the resources of the nonprofit so that community needs are met. Such Communitarians manage to join planning committees or boards of nonprofits. They stay actively involved in nonprofits to ensure that results are achieved. Communitarians need periodic feedback from the nonprofit that their motivations for giving (local causes, solid management, opportunity to interact with other business leaders) are recognized and addressed. They like the type of individualized attention and responsiveness they are used to as heads of business enterprises.

Some Communitarians Want to Influence How Donations Are Used

A higher proportion of Communitarians than any other philanthropic personality (41.8%) feel they should have a say in just how their contributions are to be used. They feel their business acumen and local knowledge qualifies them for important ongoing advisory roles.

> I know my community, and I know what should be done here. I have a right to give my opinion where my money should go, and where the Lion's Club overall should make the effort.

> I grew up here all my life. Who has a better feel for the neighborhood? Who has a better understanding of how to use money to make a difference than a successful businessman who knows just about everyone?

Moreover, these Communitarians have a need to see that the nonprofit is being run productively. In this way they create a sense of security that their monies are being used effectively.

> I have to believe it's being run like a business. I run my business by paying attention to the details, they should do the same thing.

Other Communitarians (58.2%), like most major donors in general, prefer to believe that the people managing nonprofits are competent to make funding and program decisions without donor input. It is important to note that Communitarians have faith in the people running nonprofits because they have personal and/or professional relationships with these individuals and carefully check out each nonprofit's record.

> I know each and every person on the board. I do business with them. I know the type of people they are. I trust them to do the right thing with the money they get.

> If I didn't have faith in the guys running the show, I would have never donated so much to them.

Communitarians Want to Be Assured That the Nonprofit Recognizes Why They Are Giving

Overall, 83.9 percent of Communitarians think it is very important that nonprofits they support recognize the reasons they are giving. Communitarians want the nonprofit to reflect back to them the themes of a win-win relationship — local support for local causes, effectiveness and efficiency in operations, and opportunities to interact with other business leaders. Communitarians expect well-run nonprofits to go out of their way to make sure donors' needs are understood.

Communitarians Expect Nonprofits to Look Out for Their Needs

Almost all Communitarians (85.7%) consider it very important that nonprofits have their best interests at heart. Communitarians expect nonprofits to be aware of all their needs and wants — from committee assignments to recognition. This expectation flows from the model of exchange Communitarians have of the basic donor/nonprofit relationship. If they are doing something for the nonprofit, Communitarians expect the nonprofit to do something for them.

> If they don't have my interests at heart and I'm making sure they stay in business, it's not realistic to believe they would be able to have their clients' interests at heart, or the symphony goers', or anyone else's.

Communitarians are highly interpersonally oriented (88.9%) and value time spent in developing and furthering relationships.

> Schmoozing is the way to go. It's the juice that makes things run. I want to be schmoozed. I want them to make the effort to get to know me and know me well. I like fund raisers to understand my life and what the town means to me.

> I grew up here with everyone else. We're just plain folk, we care about each other. I have great relationships with fund raisers who relate to me personally, who talk to me about what's important to me — my family, the community, and running a business.

Communitarians Would Like Individualized Attention

Most Communitarians (86.9%) expect to receive ongoing and personal attention from fund raisers and other officers of any nonprofit they contribute significant sums to. Communitarians want tokens of appreciation, frequent updates on events, invitations to be honored, people to call with questions or suggestions. They want responsiveness to any inquiry or suggestion they would make. The kind of treatment they are used to is that of a very successful business owner.

> I'm doing this (contributing) to help my neighborhood, but frankly, I am touched and pleased any time they go out of their way to appreciate me for it.

The trustees and the staff of the boys club are great to work with. I just have to pick up the phone to get something done or a question answered. It feels like they can't do enough for me, and I appreciate that.

Communitarians Want Public Acknowledgment

Because of the close relationship between their business and personal interests, Communitarians are generally interested in public acknowledgment of their philanthropy. They want recognition in their local community and they desire publicity.

I do a lot for the Rotary Club and the other organizations (nonprofits), and while I don't tell them I expect anything, I really appreciate it when they give me some recognition. It means something when my neighbors are aware of the ways I help.

I give for a lot of reasons, but let me tell you that the publicity doesn't hurt. A public thank-you makes me feel good, and, frankly, it doesn't hurt business either.

Communitarians especially value recognition and honors from their peer group of other business owners.

When I received the Chamber of Commerce award for my charitable activities in the community, I felt so good all over. Everybody I respected said that what I was doing was great and showed them what charity meant. Ever since then, every year, I rededicate myself to the charity work I do.

Summary

Communitarians are local people made good. They support local nonprofits because it helps out the community and because it also helps out their business interests. This makes them highly approachable by community-oriented nonprofits who also meet their businesslike standards of management and operations. Communitarians will look before they leap

into a relationship with a nonprofit, and even employ a professional to help them make that assessment.

Once committed, they look for long-term relationships
and substantial involvement in nonprofit decision making,
provided they receive the type of personal attention and
recognition they desire. This includes an empathetic understanding of their motivations for giving as well as the appropriate social recognition, which is highly prized by their peer
group of local successful business owners.

2

The Devout:
Doing Good Is God's Will

Thanks to the Almighty, I have the means to improve the lives of others. I believe God intends for me to help the deserving.

All of God's children are given special talents. We must each use these talents to do his work here on Earth. One of my talents is commerce. I can make money. I have to use this talent to do God's work. That's what charity is about.

Who Are the Devout?

The Devout make up the second largest group (20.9%) of major donors. The Devout are motivated to support nonprofits for religious reasons; they say they believe that it is God's will for them to help others or that the moral teaching of their religion charges them to support charities. As a result, they channel almost all their giving (95.8%) to religious institutions and associated organizations. The Devout are mostly male (84.2%), owners of businesses (81.3%), and college educated (85.7%).

Why the Devout Give

This section offers several answers.

The Devout Give Because Giving Is a Religious Act

The Devout give because there is symmetry between the gifts they believe they have received from God (their wealth) and the gifts they, in turn, can give to others (their charity). They attribute their material success to God and recognize the need to do what they view as God's work in order to reciprocate.

> The Lord gave me a gift, the gift of making money. He gave me this gift so I can share it with other people.

> My good fortune is the benevolence of the Almighty. My benevolence is just another form of His.

Charitable behaviors are religiously fulfilling for the Devout. They feel they are conforming with key principles in their belief systems. Their motivation to be philanthropic is an integral component of their religious orientation. Many quote religious scriptures to explain their motivations.

> I guess I do quote the Bible a lot, but you have to understand that's what makes it all important to me. The Bible is God's words and those words tell us to love one another. That is what charity means—to show that we love one another.

> It is better to give than to receive. When I'm in synch with teachings like that, I can do more for myself and others. As a result, I am a better person.

In addition, for the Devout, the act of giving itself is a sign of spiritual development and maturity. For the Devout, every good deed represents a positive step in their personal spiritual development, and significant philanthropy reflects on a largess of soul.

Religious growth—that's what life is all about. When I give to charity, and when I get into the trenches and get dirty by volunteering, I am growing in the Spirit. Charity is essential, if people want to grow spiritually.

Philanthropy is, for me, a cornerstone of my religious education. It is at the heart of what it means to be a good Christian.

Like Communitarians, the Devout tend to restrict their giving to a certain category of causes; for the Devout it is causes that have a solidly religious orientation. Unlike Communitarians, however, these causes are not restricted to local organizations. Quite a few of the Devout contribute to international religious causes, to outreach, and to missionary work.

The Devout Give Because It Is a Moral Obligation

The Devout believe that charitable behavior is a moral imperative. They believe that all people, regardless of income and wealth, are morally obligated to do what they can to support worthy causes. In the Devout worldview, everyone should feel responsible for trying to better society. For the Devout personally, giving to charity is an inescapable moral obligation and their responsibility as good religious individuals.

The love of Jesus is the love of man. It is all our job to show that love every way we can. Then we all have to work together to make life more wonderful—and that means the wealthy must do their part and help the poor and the poor must do their part to help themselves.

My money comes from the Lord. Abraham was blessed with riches by the Lord, and so was Solomon. As he blesses us (the wealthy) we must share our good fortune with those not so fortunate. That goes for everyone. Some blessings are not monetary. There's health and family. So, as long as you are blessed, you must share your good fortune with the less fortunate.

Although the responsibility for charitable behavior is universal, the Devout do think the wealthy should shoulder a greater share of the burden because of their greater financial resources. The thought is that those who are able to do more, for whatever reason, should.

> Jesus said, "How hard is it for those who have riches to enter the Kingdom of God?" If you have riches it is especially important that you share them. If you do not, you must share of yourself. Either way, you must devote your life to the Lord's work. Money is not the issue.

> I have been blessed in many ways and that means money too. It is only right that I share my blessings with others. Wealthy people need to be more generous because they can be — it's really very simple.

The Devout Give Because It Is Good to Be Selfless

Like Altruists, the Devout resist any suggestion that charity is an exchange of some sort. Few (11.1%) agree with a statement that people give because they receive some benefit in return. The Devout believe that charitable giving should be done out of pure motives, and the purest motive is selflessness.

> Charity should be a mitsvah. If charity is not done freely without any strings attached, then I would question whether it was a mitzvah, whether it was really charity, or just some slick business move.

> Jesus never asked for anything. So, charity is about giving out of love without expecting anything in return. Charity is caring for your fellow man because that's the Christian way. Anything less cannot, in good conscience, be called charity.

> Doing God's work is what we all must concentrate on. Contributing to nonprofits, in His name, is being philanthropic. Contribut-

ing and then getting something because you contribute is not philanthropy.

Because of these views, the Devout look down upon individuals who give with an exchange of benefit in mind, or whose motives are not completely selfless. While the Devout understand that many donors expect benefits in return from nonprofits, and that many nonprofits supply these rewards, the Devout would not call it charity.

People give for all sorts of reasons. Still, you have to separate giving the way I and my friends do it from the way other people do it. We give from the heart without asking for anything in return. They give with a hidden agenda in mind. What we do is charity. What they do is business.

I think they should change the laws some way. You should only get the tax deduction if your gift is true philanthropy. When it is part of something else, like your business, you shouldn't receive the same benefits.

The Devout Give Because the Government Does Not Support Religious Causes

A large majority of the Devout (86.7%) believe they are better instruments of giving than the government for several reasons. The first is that, in the United States, the government's priorities are not religious priorities, and if religious goals are important, they are best pursued through the religious system, not the political one. The Devout with this point of view believe that individual members of government may be good people but the political system prevents them from acting morally in all cases.

The government is not some solid block of granite. There are many people that make up the government. And, it depends on who is running the show. The same is true of all the nonprofits. It depends on who's running the show. If that person is of the right frame of mind then they'll do the right thing. It really depends on the person in charge.

> I only vote for people with the strong religious convictions like me. Then I know they'll do what they can to meet the needs of society.

The second reason for skepticism is a worry that government, by its nature, is immoral because the people in government do not all share religious beliefs and values. The Devout are well aware that many policymakers do not share their religious orientation.

> The government is secular. Some people in the government are atheists. How can the government possibly do God's work? We have to do that work.

> I support nonprofit organizations being managed in accordance with true Christian values because the government does not.

> It's a matter of morals. Most of the charities I give to have a firm moral foundation. The same can't be said about this country's government. Lots of politicians talk about family values, but I don't think many politicians live moral lives.

How the Devout Select Nonprofits

Because honesty and trust are valued so highly in the religious belief systems of the Devout, they generally take the claims of a charitable cause on faith if it is endorsed by or closely associated with the religious organization. Compared to the other philanthropic personalities, the Devout say they are less likely to conduct a protracted or extensive personal investigation of the organization.

The Devout Make Giving Decisions Based on Trust

Among all the Philanthropic personalities, the Devout are least likely to scrutinize a giving decision. Less than half

(44.2%) of the Devout say they spend a great deal of time and effort evaluating the nonprofits they donate to. The Devout focus the least on evaluating nonprofits because the ones they donate to tend to be religiously oriented. The Devout prefer to give on trust to people and organizations sharing their beliefs and moral outlook.

> You have to have faith. That also means having faith in the church and its ministers. They are doing what needs to be done and there isn't any need to look over their shoulders.

> I give to my church. There just isn't any question of the integrity of the church and what it does.

However, there is a trend of increasing skepticism toward even religious fund raising. The many scandals that have plagued religious fund-raising institutions in recent years have made even the Devout somewhat more guarded.

> Look at all the televangelists. They're proof you can't just give to the Church and not pay attention to just who you are giving your money to.

> Ever since the Calvi affair with the Vatican bank, I feel I can't just give to the Catholic Church and assume everything will be as it should. Now I take the time to find those people who are doing something worthwhile and those who are not.

The Devout Do Not Rely on Professional Advisors

The Devout do not generally use advisors to help them make charitable decisions. Either their donations are directed at an institution they are intimately familiar with, within their own religious community, or the funds are directed at an organization with high credibility.

> I know who to give to because I know why to give. I give to further the good work of the church, so I give to the church. I certainly don't need any help in making that choice.

It isn't necessary to ask for anyone's opinion. I give to do God's work, so I give to the church. There just isn't any question about who to donate to.

The few Devout who did utilize a philanthropic advisor (12.5%) said they simply turned to their spiritual mentor for assistance. For them, these decisions are the same as any other spiritual matter which might require appropriate guidance.

The rabbi understands God's words; he is such a learned man. He helps me to think about how best to serve the Lord. The rabbi helps me to decide how to do the most good when I donate to charity.

I look to the church for guidance in my life and this includes how to donate money. Not only do I give to the church, I also give to other causes — and the church helps me with those decisions too.

What the Devout Look for After the Gift

Because of the high credibility of the charitable institutions they support, the Devout do not usually seek much influence over how donated funds are used. The Devout seldom become highly involved in policy-making in the nonprofits they donate to. The Devout are also generally indifferent to recognition and honors, since they believe that the real rewards operate on a spiritual level. Only when recognition comes within their peer group context do they find it meaningful.

Influencing the Use of Donated Funds

Less than a quarter (24.4%) of the Devout believe they should take an active role in determining how the money is used after they donate it. Generally, the Devout base their giving decisions on trust and believe that assumption of trust should continue. Acting on trust validates the choice of the nonprofit and the individuals who manage it.

In following His way, I give without reservations. I don't need to look over the shoulders of others. I just know they will be guided to do the right thing.

This perspective translates into an approach supportive of the individuals managing the nonprofit. For the most part, the Devout have a high implicit trust of those who share their religious orientation; this translates into a high degree of confidence in the organizations themselves. They feel it is unnecessary to become extensively involved in the policy-making or in the day-to-day operating decisions. However, the Devout like to feel that they make themselves available to provide assistance whenever needed.

Blasphemy is present in our lives when we divorce ourselves from our actions. We do not give birth to children and then let them be. They need guidance. It's the same for nonprofit organizations — we must provide guidance, but only when asked. Nonprofit organizations are not children. We should provide guidance only when asked.

Humanistic feeling requires working with charities to do God's will. You and I must not forsake our moral responsibilities or project the illusion of charity by simply giving money. We must give of ourselves when we are called upon to do so. We must give of our blood, our soul when we are called upon to do so. We must offer ourselves and when we are called upon we must come through. We are not there to impose. We must be there when we are asked.

The Devout who do want more active roles have obtained seats on boards or planning committees or are involved in the organization operations. These Devout explain their actions in terms of stewardship.

I can't only give cash and then walk away. We have more to give; we have skills and abilities that have value and it is our God given responsibility to exercise those skills and abilities in his name.

I would be shirking my moral responsibilities if I didn't take a hand in the way His charities work.

I got on the board so that I could make certain the direction of the nonprofit kept steady. I made this commitment of my time because it is important to take a leadership role in cases like this — it's God's will.

The Devout Want Nonprofits to Reflect Their Religious Values

Of all the philanthropic personalities, the Devout are most likely (95.6%) to want the nonprofits they support to recognize why they are giving and to honor the same values. The Devout have a high need for their religiously based motives to be known and understood for what they are, and to be shared by members of the nonprofit.

I give because of the benevolence God has shown me. The church groups I support appreciate my benevolence and charity, and the people who are helped by the outreach see benevolence expressed to them. It is important to me that we all see and understand benevolence the same way.

Life is the connections of me to you, you to me, one-to-one, and the Lord is with us all the time. The stronger and more frequent those connections, the more life is felt. I want to have those connections with every human being doing God's work. I want to empathize with the members of the Church and the other charities I support. And, no less important, I want them to have it with me too.

The Devout Expect the Nonprofit to Look Out for Them

The Devout unanimously feel that the nonprofit should have their best interest at heart. They see this as the logical extension of the teachings of their various religions, and of their own philosophy and actions. By taking care of an organization through giving, they expect the organization to take care of their interests in return. Because this reciprocity is based on religious beliefs, it is not the same as a commercial exchange in the minds of the Devout. Instead, mutual caring is a moral obligation.

> The interest of the Church is the true spiritual development of everyone. I take care of the church through my giving, and the church takes care of me in many ways. As a parishioner, of course the Church has my best interests at heart.

> Love thy neighbor. My pastor—my spiritual leader—looks out for all his children, and that includes me. The organizations I give, that I look out for, well, they look out after me too, and I am grateful.

As a result of this perspective, 80.2 percent of the Devout expect to receive individual attention. However, they define the concept of individual attention differently than other philanthropic personalities do. They have a very egalitarian perspective. For the Devout, individual attention is equated with the consideration nonprofit personnel are expected to provide to everyone—not just them, not just the nonprofit's clients, not just the public, but everyone.

> We are all God's children. We all therefore deserve love and respect. It is the Church's role to demonstrate caring for everyone—those who are served by the social programs and those who make it possible for the Church to have those social programs.

> Jesus teaches us to love each one another. So, to show love we must be responsive to each other as unique—there's the need for individual attention.

The Devout do admit having some desire to be recognized and held up for their good work, but they want any personal credit for good works kept within their religious organization. They are, however, anxious that the nonprofit organization receive broad public appreciation of and recognition for its works.

> It's part spiritual and part moral life — philanthropy is. In the Scriptures it is written that we love each other, because this is right, not because we get a fancy plaque. It's nice to get an award, but that's not the cause for a spiritual and moral life. That's a result. The awards are all right so long as we never get confused about why we are doing the good work.

> I was deeply honored when my parish gave me the philanthropist of the year award. I have done volunteer work for years. I have always contributed heavily. It's great that I got the award but it's even greater that the parish received the recognition it deserves. I am always willing to do everything in my power to help the parish in any way I can.

Summary

Everything about the Devout stems from their deep religious orientation. Since they attribute their affluence to a gift from God, they feel a deep desire to share that gift with others within their religious community. In the minds of the Devout, the gift of philanthropy is to be shared in the same way it came — selflessly, uncritically, trustfully. The Devout expect to be treated well by the nonprofit. However, they insist this treatment be grounded equally in religious and moral motives to strive to treat all people well, and not emanate from any felt obligation to reciprocate. The Devout do not mind recognition, as long as it is small-scale and kept within the religious community.

3

The Investor:
Doing Good Is Good Business

It's not a question of whether to give or not. It's a question of how to do it so that I'm not doing something financially dumb. I want to be smart about the financial aspects of how I give.

Giving only makes sense when everyone comes out winning. This way the positive relationships can continue to be positive and continue for a good long time. If I don't consider the financial repercussions of giving, my charitable relationships will not be very strong for very long.

Who Are Investors?

Investors are donors who give with one eye on the cause of the nonprofit and one eye on personal tax and estate consequences. About 15.3 percent of major donors are Investors. A typical Investor is a well educated (84.1% have a college degree) male (86.7%) head of household who provides for his family through the ownership of a business (74.5%). Business-owning Investors seek to prepare for their family's future security through the smooth transfer of the business assets and farsighted estate planning. Investors are interested in doing good along the way through a well conceived and executed

43

program of donating to nonprofits that is keyed to their financial plan. Investors donate to a wide range of nonprofits and are the segment most likely to support umbrella nonprofits such as community foundations (22.4%).

Why Investors Give

Investors give because they are financially able to do so, because they have a personal desire to do good works, and because they possess enough business acumen to give in a businesslike way. They apply the same careful analysis to their nonprofit contributions as they do to any investment. Moreover, they think of giving and of investing in much the same terms.

Investors Give the Same Way They Invest

For Investors, the financial benefits associated with donating sets the parameters of their philanthropic behavior. While Investors want to benefit society, their specific funding decisions take their personal financial situation into careful consideration.

> I carefully look at my balance sheet, and, with my accountant, figure out just how much I should give away. It is not a matter of whether to give, I am certainly going to give. It is really a matter of how much to give, what is the best way to give, and to whom.

> I always give and I always will. At the same time, I have to make sure it works for me and my family. That's why I have to include a solid look at my financials whenever a giving decision has to be made.

Because Investors view their contribution as an investment, at least in part, they tend to engage in inventor-like behaviors with respect to nonprofits. This is equivalent to a Wall Street analyst evaluating the quality of a company before deciding whether or not to purchase the stock.

I scrutinize the charities I give to as much as I do anywhere else I put my money. This way, I am confident my money is being used the way it's supposed to be.

The way things are nowadays, you have to be very careful, even when giving to charities. The only way to be sure you're doing something useful is to shop around so you can get the most return on that dollar.

Investors Structure Giving for Tax Advantages

Investors tend to believe that much, if not all, the monies they give nonprofits would otherwise be diverted to government in the form of taxes. Tax avoidance alone is a powerful motivator to this group, and a significant stimulus to their philanthropic behavior. In addition, Investors tend to agree that government spending can be wasteful and that the government does not always use tax revenues wisely. As a result, they feel that charitable actions taken by individuals are more beneficial to society than are efforts made by the government.

Either you get a say in where your money goes by using the tax system to give it away to charity, or you don't and just give it in taxes to the government. Either way, your money is going to go. By giving to charity, you can get a say, so you should.

It's like when I set up a charitable trust. It was explained to me so clearly. When I go, my family will get half the estate. The rest of my estate will either go to the IRS or to a charity of my choosing. Once it was explained like that, there wasn't any question. For my money, the IRS is going to lose out, and the charity is going to win.

Investors do not have rose-colored glasses on about nonprofits; they tend to be critical and to find faults and shortcomings. But, when confronted with the choice about which sector—government or nonprofit—is relatively more capable and efficient, Investors give the nod to nonprofits.

I get rather heated about this. It's almost as though the government takes precious metals and transforms them into base metals. High quality nonprofits, to my mind, do just the opposite; they can take lead and turn it into gold. I want to make lead into gold, not the other way around.

No one can say with a straight face that our government is well run these days. Nonprofits are run better, and between the two I'd pick nonprofits every time.

A sizable majority of Investors (71.9%) agree that nonprofits are superior to the government in dealing with the problems confronting society. Investors emerge as the philanthropic personality most questioning of government and its use of tax monies.

I pay a fortune in taxes, and it doesn't amount to a thing. The government seems to fritter money away. At least when I give to charities, I'm the one who picks where my money goes, and I can give to well run charities. Because of that I feel I'm doing more by giving to charity.

The fed, the state, the county, the city—collect loads of taxes and give the money away. They are very, very good at it. But for all that money, things don't seem to be better. For my money, charity can make things better.

However, quite a few Investors are highly critical of both sectors. Skepticism runs deep in this philanthropic personality, and some Investors view nonprofits as the lesser of two evils. The more thoughtful Investors know they have to select nonprofits carefully, and rely on the quality of the people in management.

I know about governmental agencies because I worked on advisory boards and I also know about nonprofits because I'm a trustee on some boards. Neither government nor nonprofits are any good in and of themselves. You have to take a good look at the people in charge. That's the only way to tell.

Investors Do Not Feel Morally Obligated to Give

Not a single Investor in the sample agreed with the statement that 'the wealthy are morally obligated to support worthy causes.' Investors do not generally feel that there are community, social, or moral pressures on them to give. Giving is not part of their lifestyle, as it is for the Communitarians, nor is it an inherent part of how they define themselves, as it is for the Devout. Instead, giving is something personally rewarding that is sanctioned by the IRS, thereby providing financial benefits as well. For Investors, giving is not mandatory in a moral or ethical sense.

> In parochial school they tried to convince us we must all do our part to make our world a wonderful place to live. But they couldn't convince me that we must do good deeds. The way I see it, if you want to, that's great. If you don't, that's OK too.

> Charity is something that comes from within. You can never impose it on anyone.

In Particular, Being Affluent Does Not Impose Moral Imperative to Give

Investors particularly resent being told that they have a moral obligation to give because of their wealth. Investors generally dismiss any notion that wealthy people have a special role to play as philanthropists. To Investors, the wish to give is either there or not there within a person. They do not believe that having wealth makes a person more or less inclined to be philanthropic, nor do they believe in any special responsibility of wealth to be charitable.

> Money isn't the critical factor. It's what you believe in that counts. If you believe strongly enough, then you will do something whether you have money or not.

> People are people. If you want to do something to help some worthy cause, you do. Otherwise, you don't. Being rich doesn't change any of this.

Investors Believe Acts of Philanthropy,
Not Motivations, Define the Philanthropist

Almost all Investors (96.9%) agree that the focus should be on the act of giving rather than on something as ephemeral as a motivation to give. Investors are results oriented and define philanthropy in the same way.

> Philosophers talk about the means justifying the ends and all sorts of philosophical mumbo-jumbo. I built my business and made my money by putting in the hours day after day. It doesn't make me more charitable or less charitable than some guy who inherits his money. If someone gives, they're a philanthropist.

> We've got to be pragmatic. The robber barons cheated a lot of people but now they're remembered as great contributors to society. I think they did it to alleviate their guilt. But it really doesn't matter why they did it, it's just good that they did do it.

Investors are skeptical that anyone is truly altruistic or selfless. They personally do not feel this way and are unable to recognize such an approach to philanthropy.

> I bet that underneath all that pious talk there are real deal makers involved in all the charities.

> It's all quid pro quo. I'll scratch your back, you'll scratch mine. You are never ever going to get away from that—it's human nature. You might put pretty bows around it, make it look good. Still, it's the same with a lot of window dressing. Anyone who tells you they're altruistic is either deceiving you or deceiving themselves.

How Investors Select Nonprofits

Conceptually, Investors think of donations to nonprofits in the same way they think of tax and investment decisions. Like those decisions, a poor or uninformed decision can have serious adverse consequences. To avoid these pitfalls, Investors are very cautious in their selection of nonprofits to support. Investors seek to mitigate the risk of giving through careful selection and planning.

Investors Plan Donations to Nonprofits Methodically

Investors do not impulsively donate to a nonprofit; instead, they prefer to do considerable research and evaluation. Most Investors (81.3%) go through a rigorous process of evaluating the efficacy of nonprofits and base a donation decision upon that assessment. Investors believe they are looking for good "returns" on their donation "investment" and treat a donating decision as they would any other business or financial decision.

> You don't want to throw away your money foolishly and you don't have time to keep on top of the charity. So, you do all you can do to make sure you pick a good one.

> I look at my giving as an investment. When I invest, I expect to see a reasonable return. Charity, to me is the same thing. If everyone who donated took the time to analyze where their money was going, like they do a stock, then we would all be much better off. Our charity investments would finally pay real dividends like better education and less crime and a cleaner environment.

As a result, Investors seek out nonprofits they believe are professionally administered. Like the Communitarians, Investors take the time to evaluate the people managing nonprofits because they are interested in obtaining results and they must depend on people to get those results.

> It's not enough to want to do good. Resources all over are limited. Therefore, nonprofits have to show me they are going to be effective. I will not give to anybody unless they can prove this to me.

> A real important cause is great. But the cause doesn't mean a thing if the management is unfocused and can't get anything

meaningful accomplished. I believe only nonprofits which have proven themselves deserve my support.

The only way for me to feel that the nonprofit is going to deliver on its promises is by looking at the quality of its management. If the people in charge are smart and capable, I feel there is a good chance the nonprofit will deliver.

Choosing a nonprofit that is the functional equivalent of a mutual fund is the way some Investors defer the intensive front-end work of evaluating each and every nonprofit opportunity. Many select umbrella organizations such as the United Way or community foundations and leave the evaluation of specific charities to those organizations.

I rely on the (community) foundation to make sure my money is not being wasted. This way, I don't have to sort through all the charities myself. They stay on top of the charities.

Relatively Few Investors Currently Use a Philanthropic Advisor, But Most Are Interested in the Concept

Only a few Investors (10.3%) used advisors in making philanthropic decisions. Those who did were satisfied with the assistance they received.

I hire consultants for my business. I hire consultants all the time for all sorts of things. I mean, I even have a gardener and a pool service. Everybody pays people to do things that are specialized. It only makes sense to hire consultants when I make important decisions like who to give my money to—and how much to give them.

To me it's very important to make sure my donations have an effect. Most of the time, there's no good way to tell what is really accomplished by even the best nonprofit. The only way for me to feel good about who I donate to is to make sure the nonprofit is a quality operation. Well, I don't know how to do a good job of evaluating them, so I hire an expert.

Investors who did not use the services of a philanthropic advisor, like the Communitarians, tended to be unaware of the existence of such professionals. Investors are generally interested in the concept, as they perceive that philanthropic advisors would reduce their risk by helping to ensure that only high quality nonprofits are supported.

> Thinking about it, I might have hired someone to help me through the process. I just didn't know the service was available.

> It's a great idea. Not only would I be willing to hire a philanthropic advisor, but I bet a lot of other people would too. That's a service I'd love to invest in.

What Investors Look for After the Gift

Investors again invoke an investment analogy to explain that they want little to do with operational decisions of the nonprofit after their donation has been made. Just as with purchasing a mutual fund, the point is selecting a team that will run the investment well and not require day-to-day intervention and management on the part of the Investor unless that kind of support is offered. Investors expect a businesslike and highly professional relationship with the nonprofit, and they also expect to be acknowledged and paid attention to.

Investors Do Not Seek Influence over Use of Funds

Very few Investors (3.1%) believe they should oversee or influence the use of the funds they contribute to nonprofits. Most Investors believe they already made that decision by selecting the type of nonprofit they did. Others say the choice of well-managed nonprofits means their oversight is not required.

> I have this utilitarian view. I want to make sure my giving gets the most mileage possible. That means picking charities well and when asked to help out on the management or policy end, I'm

there to do whatever I can, but I'd rather choose charities that are well run and stand back.

I influence the way the charity uses my contribution but I do it in an indirect sort of way. I do it when I choose who to contribute to. I only pick charities which have a track record of success, and then I don't interfere.

Investors Expect Nonprofits to Understand Their Business Concerns

A considerable majority of Investors (87.5%) felt it extremely important that nonprofits understand them and their motives for giving. Investors especially want nonprofits to understand them as businesspersons. For example, Investors' affluence generally derives from their businesses, and changing business conditions can materially affect their ability to be generous with nonprofits. Investors resent it when nonprofits press for additional support without being sensitive to the business realities facing their donors.

> These guys just don't get the connection between my firm's performance and my giving to charity. It would be refreshing if they showed a little of the concern for us donors that they show to the homeless.

> It has to be financially feasible for me to be very generous. Now, don't get me wrong, I always give. But, the big money has to be in those years when the company does real well.

Investors also expect nonprofits to interact with them in a businesslike way, which in their minds means emphasis on numbers and results. Anything less than a financial and operations-driven bottom-line focus only conveys a lack of business management skills which Investors find highly unattractive. With Investors, nonprofits need to communicate and emphasize the financial and business fundamentals of the organization.

When I deal with a nonprofit organization, I expect them to know what's important, important in a business sense, so I do not waste my time.

When they ask me for more money, they had better be talking about the quality of their programs and they better be able to prove those programs are top notch. The do-good stuff without numbers just irritates me all get out and it's not going to make me interested in giving.

I'm always on the lookout for charities where the directors really do make the effort to understand that I'm concerned about a proven track record of results, not some promises.

Investors Want Nonprofits to Look Out for Their Interests, But Want Reassurance That Constituents Are Not Shortcut

Most Investors (87.5%) consider it very important that the nonprofit have their best interests at heart. Not necessarily just because Investors want the attention, but because having a customer's interest front and center is good business practice, and Investors think of themselves as customers in the relationship.

I look for them to be in synch with me after I spent a lot of time with them, and I assume that if they are treating me well, then they are treating the people they help well, too.

In my business we had a motto: the customer always comes first. It is the same way with nonprofits; I expect to be treated as a customer. I expect to be treated right.

Some Investors have had less than satisfactory experiences with nonprofits on this basis. Some Investors feel their motivations, constraints, and needs have been misunderstood by nonprofits.

> I explained to everybody I normally give to that the recession
> has been a bear and that I just don't have the money I did the
> year before. One of them didn't seem to care and kept asking
> for support. Frankly, I resented it.

Investors are not initially concerned about a close interpersonal relationship with officers of the nonprofit. In the
beginning of an association, Investors define empathy as a nonprofit's awareness of the donor's personal situation so they can
interact on a businesslike basis. Over time, however, interpersonal dynamics become increasingly important to Investors.

> In the beginning I wanted them to know when they can ap-
> proach me about something and when to hold back. I didn't really
> want to be too friendly. But now, years later, we're all buddies.
> It just took us some time.

Investors Want Public and
Private Acknowledgment and Attention

Most Investors (90.6%) rate individual attention as very important to them. The interest of Investors in receiving personal attention is consistent with their motivations for giving. Since Investors have a great respect for money, and for
the amounts they give away, they expect this generosity to
be acknowledged. In the minds of Investors, such a response
is only normal business procedure.

> I appreciate it when charities go out of their way to make sure
> I know my efforts are appreciated.

> Frankly, if I don't receive personal attention and appreciation,
> then I start to question the professionalism of the organization,
> and then I start to question if supporting the organization is a
> good idea or not.

Investors desire appropriate formal recognition for their
charitable behavior, and they believe formal recognition

should be given to individuals who have been demonstrably beneficial to a nonprofit. Honors awarded too lightly are not seen as particularly valid.

I've been given two award dinners in my name so far. The first one was for a charity I wasn't that much involved with, and I felt I didn't really deserve it. Now, the second time I was the honoree, that was special. I spent five years first as a volunteer on a few committees, then as a board member. I sweated literally and figuratively for that place. I did deserve that honor and I was delighted to get it and show it off in my office. It's a great conversation piece. It helps me get some of the guys I do business with to also become involved. I'm real proud of it and the charity.

I think it's only worthwhile to honor people who have made a noticeable difference. I get aggravated when it feels like it's for diddly stuff. Groups have tried to honor me plenty of times, and I only accept if I think I deserve it.

Summary

Investors approach the nonprofit interaction principally as a business relationship. The size and timing of major donations is driven by business results as well as tax and estate considerations. Investors spend considerable effort assuring themselves that a given nonprofit is sufficiently well managed to make a suitable target for their generosity. In return, Investors expect nonprofits to behave in businesslike ways, such as being results oriented, and acknowledging major donors in the same way business owners cater to major customers.

4

The Socialite:
Doing Good Is Fun

It is wonderful to be able to bring people together socially who can make a difference by supporting charity.

We all work together, my friends and I, to raise money for charity. When one of us decides to help a charity, that charity gets all of us. It's a team effort.

Who Are Socialites?

Extroverted, gregarious Socialites desire to help through being active in charity work, and they rely on their close friends and family to assist them in being effective. Socialites find social functions benefiting nonprofits to be an especially appealing way to help make a better world and have a good time doing it. They make up 10.8 percent of major donors.

Socialites are principally women (62.3%) who have college degrees (79.1%) and whose source of wealth is commonly the privately owned businesses managed by their spouse (74.7%). Socialites tend to support nonprofits which offer more opportunities for socializing, such as the arts and education, as well as religious nonprofits.

Why Socialites Give

Socialites give because they are members of a social class for which many entertainments have a fund-raising aspect. This fund-raising aspect legitimates the entertainments themselves in the eyes of Socialites. In addition, the process of putting on a large event provides them with the means to develop an extensive support and social network of like-minded people which can be tapped again and again to further philanthropic and social goals.

Socialites Relish Creating Enjoyable Ways for Others to Give

Socialites are attracted to the social circle which surrounds nonprofits, to the entertainments themselves and, most importantly, to doing good in the process.

> It's more than just the parties. It's the opportunity to help those who need assistance and to support great cultural centers together with people who have the same interests and concerns as you do.

> Everyone does things in ways that work for them. Being part of the group lets me have an effect and I can even enjoy myself along the way.

Socialites are not merely interested in the social interactions and social status which they create as a result of their philanthropy. Rather, Socialites express a desire to be constructively philanthropic and are attracted to a particular social milieu which serves as their philanthropic platform. While Investors strive to make their philanthropic decisions based on an investment paradigm, Socialites refer to a social paradigm.

> I wanted to do something worthwhile, but I didn't know what to do. It wasn't until I began going to charity functions that I

found people who looked at things like I do. I wanted the support of a group to help me do something worthwhile.

Fitting in socially is all based on who you know and that means networking. The best place to network is at the planning meetings for the galas. That's my intelligence system, and my support system, my contact system and now they are my friendship system.

Socialites Give Because They Can Direct
Their Giving to Places the Government Overlooks

Like Communitarians, Socialites have highly developed networks in their local communities. Socialites believe that, because of this special local knowledge, they know better than governmental agencies where the needs are. Almost all Socialites (91.7%) agree that the nonprofits they support are far more capable of dealing with the needs of society than government is at this time. Their behaviors are consistent with these attitudes. In their day-to-day dealings, Socialites tend to be highly involved in nonprofits and uninvolved with governmental agencies. In addition, Socialites believe their informal network, which is composed of well-connected and highly motivated individuals like themselves, is well suited to identifying needs overlooked by the government. They act to fill those gaps.

Sometimes it seems as though they (government agencies) don't know where they're at. They have no real contact with the people who need the help. They don't seem to be able to do anything about problems like the environment or like school children or like AIDS or even those who don't have a job. It seems to me that we need people with their hand on the pulse of the community, people like Sue Ann and Clara and Robert and me, who are doing something about these problems at the local level, doing something important. We're on the real important charities and we know what's important.

My friends and I feel that when you are involved in charity work you get a real good feeling for what matters. Once you understand what matters, you can figure out what to do about it. The government is too far away.

Socialites Can Feel Defensive About Their Socially Oriented Way of Doing Good

Socialites are aware that they have been stereotyped and criticized for the social benefits they derive from their charitable efforts. They feel such criticism is unjustified, and point to all the money that is raised and all the good that is done as a result of their efforts. Because of recurring criticisms, Socialites are particularly concerned that any nonprofit with which they are affiliated have a sterling reputation and a track record of visible and positive results.

Some people think it's all about exclusive big parties. That bothers me, so let me tell you, because of those big parties, the fine arts center is here, the hospital has a neonatal unit, and there's a half-way house in town. I can go on and on. Those big parties raise money—piles of money. Without them there would be a lot less good going on.

I don't pay much attention to people who attack the charity ball scene. They only see the balls, they never see where the money goes and the good it does.

Socialites Give Because They Are Charitable at Heart and Happen to Have Money

Socialites do not believe that they are philanthropic because they have money and are able to give some away. Instead, they believe that philanthropic behavior is part of their personality, and that having wealth just allows them to express this side of their personality in the way they do.

> We figure that we give because we believe in what we are do-
> ing. It has nothing to do with social responsibility or such. Be-
> ing richer doesn't make you any more or less responsible. It's
> not like with the money you now have to be a different person
> than what you have always been.

> Being wealthy doesn't make a difference to me. If I didn't have
> money, I would find another way to do good. I was always charita-
> ble and I always will be. The money has nothing to do with it.

Socialites believe the reverse is true as well—that the
mere fact of having money does not obligate anyone to give.
According to most Socialites, the philanthropic impulse has
to rise from within.

> Just because I have money doesn't mean I now have to contrib-
> ute a lot to charity. Money doesn't make the difference in some-
> body's character.

> Being charitable has to be something that comes from deep in-
> side. It has nothing to do with having money or not. I was al-
> ways a giving person even before I had money. Back then I gave
> my time. Now, I still give my time and I can also give money.

Socialites Believe That the True Way to Look at Philanthropy Is by What It Accomplishes

By and large, Socialites do not mind if their motives are
scrutinized; they are comfortable with why they give. They
do agree, however, that the more productive way for givers,
nonprofits, and the world at large to view philanthropy is to
focus on results, on the good it does. Focusing on results
makes the reasons one person or another gives irrelevant, and
the processes by which they give irrelevant as well. Over
three-quarters of Socialites (79.2%) agree with the statement
that the act of giving is more important than the reason for
giving.

We give and we all realize that we're making a difference. It doesn't matter just why we do it — though in my case, it's because I'm real concerned — so long as we contribute.

A baby cries because he's hungry. And, the baby doesn't care why a big person comes along to feed him, just that he does. Charities don't care why I give. They're hungry for the money and I come along and give. They get what they need. That's what's important.

How Socialites Select Nonprofits

Because of the significant social consequences of being affiliated with one nonprofit or another, Socialites are extremely careful in choosing which nonprofits to support.

Socialites Select Nonprofits Carefully and Choose Only Those That Are Approved by Their Social Network

Because Socialites are so focused on the results of their helping, they devote time and energy up front to insure that the causes they back are appropriate. Socialites generally (79.2%) consider it very important to carefully evaluate the nonprofits they support. For Socialites, support extends far beyond the giving of a donation or the establishment of a trust. Socialites, by their nature, become highly involved in the demanding work of creating and managing social affairs which are fund raisers for the nonprofit. To make these affairs successes, they call on their network of other Socialites to support their cause by serving on committees, buying tables, and attending the functions. This social exchange process will only work effectively if the chosen nonprofit is itself so respectable, compelling, and well run that it presents no social risk to be affiliated with it.

There are a lot of worthy causes out there. You can't help everyone. You have to concentrate on one. That's what makes a laser

beam different then a flashlight, concentration. Picking a charity for me is changing what I do from a flashlight to a laser
beam—I concentrate. So, I spend a lot of time picking out just
which charities I will concentrate on.

If it's going to work, I have to be very confident about the nonprofit organization I'm going to be associated with. It has to be
acceptable to all the people I deal with because they're the ones
I'm going to ask for support. That's why I take my time and really
check things out before I commit myself to any nonprofit organization.

Socialites' selection processes are similar to their donating process; they rely on their extensive network. In other
settings, such word-of-mouth networks have been called referral networks, and they are powerful forces in determining individual choice. In this case, Socialites reduce their social risk significantly by relying on their social network to
help them narrow down the set of nonprofits to support.
Since Socialites turn to these same social contacts when
they engage in fund raising, selecting a nonprofit that others
will support is a critical task. By relying on their social networks to approve the nonprofit before becoming actively
involved, Socialites are ensuring success for their fund-raising
efforts.

I am very interested in which charity is doing the best job,
although I don't have the time or even the know-how to figure
it out. So, I turn to my friends to find out. Then, I give to where
I know I can get others to support me, so my contributions will
have the biggest bang for the buck.

By making sure everyone thinks a particular charity is a top line
operation doing needed worthwhile things, I know I can go back
to them when I have to raise money. They already tacitly told
me they would support it.

Some Socialites Use Philanthropic Advisors in Helping Them Sort Through Nonprofits

Although heavily influenced by their peers in determining which charities to support, Socialites also seek to be highly effective in their giving behavior. As a result, some turn to professional advisors for assistance. One fifth (20.0%) of Socialites utilize the services of philanthropic advisors when making charitable decisions. Philanthropic advisors are intimately familiar with the nonprofit sector and are attuned to the social circles Socialites inhabit.

> I take in what everyone says. But, that doesn't tell me enough. I mean I just don't feel comfortable giving away so much money without having some experts go over these things with me. So, I just review the choices with my lawyer.

> I hired a real pro to help me make decisions. I'm the one who has the final say. It's all a matter of not making a mess of it all. Since I hire pros for everything else, why not hire a pro when it comes to making such important decisions—the who's and how's of making charitable donations.

The majority of Socialites (80.0%) still do not consider it necessary to hire a philanthropic advisor, believing that such professionals cannot add to what is already known among the Socialite network. By properly utilizing their social contacts, the majority of Socialites feel they can obtain all the information they need to make viable philanthropic decisions.

> All you have to do is keep your eyes and ears open. This way you'll be able to make intelligent decisions. It's not necessary to have to pay someone to tell you what your friends know.

> The idea sounds good and I guess a philanthropic advisor would be useful if you weren't very well connected. I don't have that problem. I have people I can call up and get the information I need whenever I need it.

What Socialites Look for After the Gift

Most Socialites like individual attention and public recognition. They appreciate being honored for their philanthropic motivations.

Socialites Are Unanimous That They Expect Individual Attention from the Nonprofit

All the Socialites consider it very important that nonprofits focus on their needs. Socialites view philanthropy as a social exchange and feel they deserve individual attention from the nonprofit officers in exchange for their efforts in fund raising.

> I just feel that it is only right for nonprofits to show me some individual attention and concern for all that I am doing for them.

> I make a big difference for the museum. Frankly, I like it that they see things the same way, and they make a big difference for me with honorary banquets and recognition in their periodicals.

Socialites define individual attention as actions by key members of the nonprofit organization designed to make them feel valued. They like it when nonprofit staff are quick to respond to their inquiries and needs. They like small tokens of appreciation. They relish public acknowledgment and attention. Socialites particularly want to be kept informed about what is going on with the nonprofits they support.

> The museum takes such good care of me; it really makes everything I do for them seem especially worthwhile. It never seems to be a problem for them to find an extra ticket when I need one or help me out in any other way.

> It is really important for me to be kept up-to-date on what's going on in the charities I support. I like hearing from the board

and the others about what is going on. It can be so embarrassing to hear about something important from a friend.

Socialites are quite clear that a lapse in attentiveness by the nonprofit will result in their withdrawing support. Socialites are also prepared to share any negative experiences throughout their referral network. As Socialites all generally expect the same type of attentive, individualized treatment from the nonprofits they support, when any one finds such treatment not forthcoming, this is quickly known to all. Thus, when a nonprofit inadvertently obtains a reputation of being unresponsive to its major donors, this reputation will dissuade other Socialites from supporting it.

It doesn't happen often, but I got involved with a charity once which had its own internal problems. I felt ignored, so I pulled out as gracefully as I could and let other people know to steer clear until they got things worked out.

Individual Attention Means Reflecting
Back to Socialites the Reasons for Their Giving

People know they are heard when the person hearing reflects back to them, or paraphrases, what has been said. Almost all Socialites (91.7%) need reassurance that they are heard, that their needs and objectives are being listened to. Those needs and objectives are as varied as the Socialites themselves, and range from information on program effectiveness to perpetuating the social circle.

He (the major gifts officer) spent so much time with me, he really got to know my reasons for helping the youth center in detail. He has been fantastic at calling me up all the time with bits of information he knows I'd be pleased to know.

I was so excited when the development director understood that I was interested in much more than just the parties. Of course, I like planning the parties, but that isn't why I do charity work. That's *how* but not *why*.

Because the social network is so important to Socialites, they are particularly sensitive to actions a nonprofit may
take that enhances or detracts from the social network as a
system. Socialites do not see themselves as individual donors,
but as fund raisers. They see themselves as fund raisers
embedded in a network of reciprocal giving to the charities
supported by other members of the network.

> The charities I work with have an excellent understanding that
> we look to each other for guidance when it comes to which cause
> to support. The charities we support have started to get together
> on their own to work out ways they could help each other — one
> is getting its printing done by another's sheltered workshop
> now — that makes us feel really good.

Socialites also want "their" charities to recognize their
special status as major givers and fund raisers, and to treat them
(just slightly) better than other members of their social network.

> Feeling special is a wonderful feeling. I like to make the non-
> profits I support feel special, and I'll confess I like it when they
> make me feel special. Frankly, that is why I am pretty careful
> to be the number one supporter of any cause I support.

Socialites Are So Focused on the Fund-Raising End and Pay So Much Attention to Selecting the Nonprofit, They Have Little Need to Be Concerned with Uses of Funds

None of the Socialites believe that they should oversee the
use of the funds they contribute to nonprofits. In large part,
this is because Socialites feel they determined the way their
money is to be used by choosing which nonprofits to support. After choosing to get involved in fund raising for a nonprofit, Socialites usually want little to do with day-to-day internal operations or deciding how the funds they donate and
raise are spent.

I know the caliber and type of programs the museum sponsors. So, I don't have to get into the trenches. I am certain that the museum will continue to produce top of the line programs.

I enjoy music and art, and I've learned lots about it all. But, I'm not like a curator or anything. They know better than me what is good and what isn't—that's what they are paid to do. I don't think we should interfere with that part of it.

Socialites Desire Formal Recognition for Their Philanthropic Activities

All of the Socialites consider it very important that they are formally honored for their charitable activities. As their giving is a function of their social milieu, they are seriously concerned with validating themselves in this environment.

I suppose everyone wants to be credited for their good works. We think that for what we do there should be some form of thank you. All the honors and plaques and names on buildings is just a very sophisticated and worldly way of saying thank you, and there is nothing wrong with that.

I give ample amounts to a fair number of charities. Some of them make a big deal of recognizing me for my generosity; others are thankful but not so open about it. Just because a charity isn't into the big affairs and awards doesn't mean it's any less worthwhile. Still, I find myself feeling so good when I receive an honor. It makes me want to do more for them. It's like saying thank you to them for saying thank you to me.

Summary

For Socialites, charitable giving and the associated fundraising activities constitute a significant component of their overall personal identity, which is a social self. For Socialites, the act of selecting a nonprofit to support is a social activity, one the Socialite will principally rely on for his or her social network. Nonprofits working with socialites need to acknowledge them as part of a donor system, rather than just interact with them as individual givers.

5

The Altruist:
Doing Good Feels Right

There is so much hurt in the world. Through my giving, I am just trying to help the little that I can. It makes my life more meaningful.

For me to continue to grow as a compassionate person requires that I care. I have to care in a way that moves things forward. For me philanthropy is a process of personal development and a way to move things forward.

Who Are the Altruists?

Altruists embody the popular perception of the selfless donor—the donor who gives out of the philanthropic impulses of generosity and empathy to worthwhile causes and who modestly "wishes to remain anonymous." This conception is not far from the truth, except that a scant 9.0 percent of all major donors fit the description.

A far greater proportion of Altruists than any other group focus their philanthropy on such social causes as the elderly and the poor. Altruists tend to be college educated (90.3%) business owners (69.9%).

Why Altruists Give

Altruists say they support nonprofits principally because it gives their life a greater sense of purpose. Altruists associate their charitable behavior with personal fulfillment; they give from within themselves. Altruists believe the act of giving should be done without thought of personal benefit, and disparage donors who view philanthropy as a social exchange in the way Communitarians or Investors, for example, do.

Altruists Give in Order to Grow Spiritually

Most Altruists associate giving behavior with spiritual development. However, their form of charitable giving is an individualistic form of spiritual development. Unlike the Devout, who seek to evolve in the context of religious teachings, Altruists seek the type of personal growth often associated with the secular humanism and human potential movements. While the Devout typically identify with a traditional religious faith, Altruists are more internally oriented and are not usually affiliated with formal religion. Their personal growth conforms to their own conceptions of spirituality and not to that of any institution.

> Giving is the path of self-actualization. I feel that by donating to worthy causes, I am doing something important.

> I am charitable because it works for me. It helps to make me more than I was before. I am expanding myself by being charitable and I am helping others. What more can you ask for?

A few Altruists make direct connections between their giving and their evolution and growth in learning and wisdom. For them, there is direct linkage between their philanthropy and their own improvement as individuals.

> In order to grow as a human being, I must act like a human being. I feel it is my duty to do everything I can to make a difference in the world today.

I think that the only way to become more of a person is to do something for other people and not just for yourself. I always want to become more.

Another Altruist explains that his contributions to environmental concerns will enable him to obtain a deeper understanding of the world and, in turn, himself.

A major goal of life is the accumulation of wisdom. Wisdom means extending beyond yourself, and you can achieve that when you heal. That's why I am working to heal the earth.

Altruists Believe Giving Is a Moral Imperative

All Altruists agree that donating to charity is a moral imperative. Alltruists believe making contributions to worthy causes should be everyone's responsibility. They hold that it is everyone's moral duty to do what they can to improve the social and physical environment.

It is an obligation of all people — white and black, tall and short, rich and poor — to help those in need. Not just the rich, but it is every single person's obligation.

I just don't mean people with money, I mean each and every person has to chip in and do their share.

If anything, Altruists believe that the person with wealth has a greater obligation. They believe that, because those with means are able to do more, they should.

We're all in this together, so we all better work together to make a difference. The richer guy should do more because he or she can do more. But that doesn't let a guy who has less off the hook, everyone should do what they can do.

Whether you have money or not you are obligated to give of yourself to improve society and the world we all live in. If you do have money you have a special obligation.

Altruists Give Because They Believe
They Are the Only True Philanthropists

Altruists, more than any other philanthropic personality, reject the idea that donations could be used to further the personal ends of the donor. To them, the essence of philanthropy is giving in a selfless manner; they do not define charity in any other way.

Not one of the Altruists (0% in this sample) believe that the act of giving is more important than the reason for that act. Indeed, they believe that such giving should be called something other than philanthropy or charity. In their view, only selfless giving, their kind of giving, is true philanthropy.

> A rose is a rose is a rose. Well, charity is charity is charity. And, there's nothing you can do about it. A tulip may be very beautiful, but it isn't a rose. Giving when you expect something in return may be very rewarding for all involved—the donor, the organization—but it's just not charity.

> If charity isn't done for the right reason, which is to get nothing at all in return, then it isn't charity. It could still be something of great value, but it isn't charity.

Altruists resent, and to some extent, disparage, donors who give in order to achieve personal objectives—such as status in the community, public accolades, or access to a social group. Although they acknowledge that such giving is inevitable, they would prefer all donors to be more like themselves.

> I don't mean to turn my nose at other kinds of donors, or sound self-righteous, but philanthropy has to take into consideration *why* someone does something. When a person has ulterior motives, they are like a bad penny, always turning up and contaminating what they touch. Even when good comes out of it, you know that it's only a matter of time before you have to pay the piper. I just can't stomach all the people who exploit the sys-

tem, and yet charities can't leave out the people who give to charity with one hand and take from them with the other.

Altruists, to an extent, expect and tolerate self-interested behavior on the part of others. They recognize that their perspective is a minority position and that nonprofits need the support of benefactors whatever their motives.

Most of the world is made up of people who are looking out for number one—themselves. It's too bad but people tell me that's just human nature.

Giving just in order to get something, even a tax deduction, is not the way I think about things. Not at all. Still, if someone is going to give a nonprofit money it would be stupid not to accept it because their motives aren't pure.

Altruists Give Because Nonprofits Are Generally Morally Superior to Government

Slightly more than half (55.4%) of the Altruists believe strongly that nonprofits are superior to the government in dealing with the needs of society. Because of their attention to motivations, these Altruists are quick to distinguish between what they see as the motivations of those in government (power) and those in nonprofits (helping others). Based on these motivations alone, Altruists believe that nonprofits are better equipped to address social problems.

A kinder and gentler nation is a bittersweet comedy. It seems like this country is managed by politicians just interested in getting re-elected. The charities, well, they're different. They're usually managed by people who want to do something of value.

Finding someone in the government who really cares is like Diogenes looking for an honest man. The different charities, at least, are run by folks who have a good heart. They care, and that's the deciding factor.

How Altruists Select Nonprofits

Compared to most other segments, instinct plays a larger role in how Altruists select nonprofits. Altruists are unlikely to work within a network or rely on professional philanthropic advisors to make a giving decision.

For Altruists, Selecting a Nonprofit Is a People Process

In making their giving decisions, Altruists pay more attention to the quality of the people in a nonprofit than to its track record. Half (50.3%) the Altruists say they do not spend a great deal of time and effort in any kind of formal evaluation of the nonprofits they support. These Altruists share a belief that, once they establish the integrity of the individuals running the nonprofit in their own minds, the rest will follow.

> I don't have the time to poke around and dissect charities. I go with the ones with people I know and which have a solid reputation.

> In the final analysis, when you give to a nonprofit, you have to trust in people. If they're basically good people, and they're doing the best they can, then that's enough. It helps no one to put everyone under a microscope.

The other half of the Altruists are more skeptical and protective. This sub-segment believes it is foolhardy to make a major donation without a thorough background check. Recent scandals in the administration of major nonprofits helped them confirm this position.

> Just look at the mess with the United Way. I used to assume the integrity of the organizations I supported. That's no longer the case. Now, I check things out a lot more than before.

> I'd like to think everyone is sincere. But, it's sort of naive to think that. Nowadays, I take the extra effort to make sure my money is going to the right charity.

Selecting a Nonprofit Is a Solo Decision for Altruists

Altruists do little of their giving in or as part of a social network. They are not enlisted by others in a social circle like the Communitarians or Socialites, but prefer to find opportunities on their own, and to make their own decisions.

> In the end, I'm doing this because it's important. I have to feel it's important — no one else. That's why I'm the decision maker.

> When I look back on the philanthropies I backed and the ones I turned down, I always have to feel that I made the choice. No one pressured me into doing anything I didn't want to. I'm completely my own person.

Altruists also make their giving decisions without major consultation with others. They do their own research and rely on their own instincts. They do not use financial advisors intensively, nor do they turn to philanthropic advisors. Not a single altruist made use of a philanthropic advisor in determining which charities to support. Because Altruists believe that giving is a personal decision, outside assistance is not required.

> I give because I want to accomplish things. Since I understand what they are, there's no need to get someone else, a professional, involved.

> For me the decision of who to give to comes from within. I have no problem deciding. I don't need any help and I don't get any.

What Altruists Look for After the Gift

Altruists want very much for their needs to be known but usually decline extensive active participation in the nonprofit after the gift. They want to be influential, but in the background.

Altruists Want Nonprofits to
Acknowledge Their Altruism

In a day when everything seems to be for sale, Altruists need
to be known for their altruism. Altruists identify strongly with
their selfless motivation for giving, and need the nonprofit
to appreciate that stance. Almost all Altruists (95.2%) consider it very important that others recognize, respect, and
acknowledge their motivation to give.

> I contribute to charity for the purest of reasons. I find it upsetting
> when people fail to recognize this. I find it especially upsetting
> when the charities misconstrue my motivations, even by accident,
> like when they ask what they can do for me, or give me something,
> or want to make a public event out of something I have done.

> I give from my heart. Something like that is what I want on my
> tombstone.

All too often, in the experience of Altruists, such pure
reasons seem to be difficult for many to accept. Altruists often
feel misunderstood and underappreciated, especially by other
donors and trustees, but even, occasionally, by nonprofits.

> People in charities sometimes have trouble because I give with-
> out wanting anything in return. A few who don't know me well
> persist in offering me awards and wanting to put my name in
> the newspapers. Frankly, if they would just accept my gifts in
> the way they are given I would be much happier.

> Why is it so hard for people to just accept that I don't want any-
> thing in return for my money? I'm not trying to buy respect or
> a pass to heaven. I never give with any strings attached.

All Altruists Want from Nonprofits Is Personal Attention, Caring, and Respect

All Altruists consider it very important that nonprofits have
their best interest at heart. Because their gift is given freely,

they are delighted by "gifts" of thoughtfulness and attention that seem to be spontaneous and freely given.

> Giving is a way to expand yourself as a person. And, giving has to be promoted in an environment of respect and caring for everyone involved. I only think it is just that my gifts of caring are returned in kind. I give my money and my time. I am pleased when charities I give to show me caring and respect.

> The nature of philanthropy is a caring for ourselves, the world, our society. I don't think I should be left out of that list.

As a consequence of these attitudes, almost all Altruists (85.1%) think they should receive individual attention from nonprofits. However, they define the concept of individual attention differently than the other philanthropic personalities. Among Altruists, individual attention is equated with the consideration and concern the nonprofit personnel are expected to provide to everyone—not just them, not just the clients of the nonprofit, not just the public, but everyone.

> Each and every person needs to do whatever he or she can to make this world a better place to live. Each of us has to learn to work with each other and that means each of us must realize that everyone has special gifts and that everyone—including you and me—are unique individuals deserving of individual attention.

> Caring for someone else because he is a person means that he should receive individual attention. I hope to receive individual attention as well, since all the charities must give individual attention to their patrons and to their clients.

Altruists Resent Ignorance of Their Needs

Altruists, perhaps because of the absence of a social network, are particularly sensitive to a mishandling of their relationship by nonprofits. This often happens when nonprofits assume they are like other major donors and treat them accordingly.

I used to give to this museum, but not anymore. They got me really annoyed when they kept offering me plaques and wanting to name things after me. None of that stuff is why I give.

There was this one charity that I would have given money to, but they kept emphasizing how being involved with them would make me a respected man in the community. That's not what I care about.

Instead, Altruists prefer a more interpersonal bond which incorporates a recognition of their motivations and attitudes. Altruists expect these interpersonal relationships to grow over time.

It's a feeling of personal realization that makes charity meaningful for me. You can't believe how appreciative I am of that, and the people at the charities are aware of what this all means to me.

I prefer to work with people who approach me as someone that doesn't have to be labeled. These are the type of people I get close to, they're the ones at nonprofits which make the whole experience valuable.

Altruists Do Not Want to Be Involved in the Operations of the Nonprofit

Only 5.6 percent of the Altruists believe that they should be involved in overseeing the use of the funds they contribute to nonprofits. Altruists stay uninvolved as an extension of their selfless motivations. For the most part, Altruists feel their role is to give and provide other assistance as needed. They do not see themselves dictating the way the funds are to be used.

The idea is to help. Charity should never be a way to buy your way into the good graces of society.

We all must work together successfully. That means we all do our own parts and that means we don't get in each other's way.

So I give them the donations and they use the money. I try to
stay out of their way.

Although Altruists tend not to be interested in the specific operations of nonprofits, they do want to ensure that
the charities are able to accomplish *their* objectives. For
Altruists, this is something of a balancing act.

It's wrongheaded to try to run the show. It's also wrongheaded
to give a considerable amount of money to a charity and say ta-
ta. There has to be a happy medium. That's where I'm at. In
the middle, making suggestions when I feel it's very important
and keeping quiet the rest of the time.

Sometimes I think I'm walking a tightrope. I need to help and
I need to let them do it their way. It's worse than raising kids.

Altruists Are Not Concerned with Formal Recognition

For Altruists, giving is a form of self-fulfillment. It has very
special meaning. The awards and social recognition are not
of great importance to Altruists.

It seems like every year they want to give me a plaque or some
such. Every year I say that I'm so pleased and thank them pro-
fusely. Each year I make them choose someone else. I want it
to be about the children, not me. I want it to be about the love
I feel and the love I give. I want it to be about life. That's what
I want, not some cold lifeless plaque.

You hear scads of rich people giving to charity to see their name
in the paper or to win some award or be the guest of honor. If
that's why they do it, so be it. It's not why I give. I don't care
about the awards and I don't have much respect for people who do.

Summary

Altruists work alone seeking personal growth and development, and they see philanthropy as a natural component of

that development. Striving for the highest morality as they define it, they view giving as a moral imperative. For the Altruist, that giving has to be pure and free of self-serving motivations. In making their giving decisions, Altruists work on their own, rarely consulting advisors or a social network. All Altruists want in return is personal attention marked by spontaneous generosity and goodwill. Altruists resent being mistaken for other philanthropic personalities, and eschew the usual rewards of nonprofits—honors, publicity, and status.

6

The Repayer:
Doing Good in Return

I was very successful, but I was never into giving to charity before. But after my wife died of breast cancer, I became heavily
involved in funding organizations that are developing new treat-
ments for cancer and in funding family support groups for cancer
patients.

I just made a major gift to the agency which fed me and provided
me with clothes when I was a child. I swore to God that if I could,
I would give some other kids the same help that someone gave
me.

Who Are the Repayers?

Repayers, who are 10.2 percent of major donors, tend to have
been constituents first and donors second. A typical Repayer
has personally benefited from some institution, often a school
or hospital, and now supports that institution out of a feeling of obligation or gratitude. Repayers concentrate their
philanthropy on medical charities and educational institutions. Repayers are male by a 2-to-1 ratio, are predominantly
business owners (76.2%), and are college educated (90.8%).

Why Repayers Give

Repayers are a clear example of the phenomenon of social exchange or reciprocity, as they give because they have received. Repayers generally focus their giving on just one or a few nonprofits.

Repayers Give Out of Gratitude

Repayers are the classic example of how a dramatic change in circumstances can be the stimulus to philanthropic behavior. A change in economic status due to the education they received in medical school or some other educational institution, a stint in a hospital cardiac intensive care unit, a child injured in an auto accident—these and other significant changes in circumstance heighten awareness of help received from others, and stimulate Repayers to acknowledge this assistance. Repayers are acutely aware of how others have helped them and feel a specific and particular obligation to repay—to help in return or help others in similar situations. Often Repayers support educational institutions where they received the education they credit with their success.

> I am a big supporter of my medical school. Thanks to my school and my professors, I am as good as I am.

> I learned self-confidence in college. I grew up in college. I owe my college a lot and that's why I support it as much as I do.

Repayers who, for instance, are heart attack survivors are likely to become hospital trustees and involved in services which benefit heart attack victims and their families. Whatever the malady, there are Repayers who, out of gratitude, support nonprofits geared toward improving the situation for others.

> I was never the charity type. When my son got cancer and he died from it, well, it changed my whole life around. I know I can never bring back my son. But the foundation I endowed is

a living tribute to his memory and will be there to ease the way for other families who, sadly, are in the same boat we were.

There's that phrase: 'Life is what happens to you when you're making other plans.' That's so true. I'm now the chairman of the local juvenile diabetes association. Finding a cure for this disease has become the most important thing in my life aside from my family. A few years ago I would have laughed if someone told me I'd be doing this. Then again, a few years ago I didn't have diabetes.

Because of the specific motivation, and the narrowness of the felt obligation, Repayers tend to support fewer nonprofits, and the nonprofits they select tend to concentrate in the same area.

The thrust of it all is payback. When a good turn is done to you, then you should do a good turn to someone else. So, those people — organizations and such — that helped me along the way deserve my help — payback. I don't give to every organization that comes along. I concentrate on giving some back to the people who helped.

Some may say I give to a bunch of charities. The way I look at it, it's all the same cause underneath. A couple groups are looking for a cure, other groups help the victims. Everything I support goes back to the same disease.

Repayers are distinct from other philanthropic personalities who also operate under the exchange model. Repayers benefit first and subsequently are philanthropic. However, for Communitarians, Investors, and Socialites, the philanthropy comes first; the business, financial, and social benefits follow.

Repayers Give Because They Believe the Wealthy Have a Special Responsibility to Give

Repayers are the only philanthropic personality that makes a distinction between the affluent and the less wealthy with respect to the moral responsibility to give. A substantial majority (87.5%) of Repayers believe it is incumbent on the affluent and the successful to contribute disproportionately to charity.

> If you can, then you should. I firmly believe that wealthier citizens just have to do more because they can.

> It's sort of like a quid pro quo arrangement. You and I know the rich owe plenty. You owe some nonprofit or charity because they helped you or someone you cared about. You owe and you need to pay up. The wealthy people, in particular, need to realize that they owe lots of people and nonprofits and charities because somewhere along the way they took and now they have to give back.

While Repayers are the only segment of affluent donors that differentiates philanthropic responsibility based on wealth, this view appears to emerge relatively late in their lives, and as a response to some event. The attitude of Repayers before they were motivated to contribute was similar to that of Communitarians, Socialites, and Investors; that is, it is an individual choice whether or not to give and there is no special obligation imposed by wealth. This shift in perspective is most evident among Repayers contributing to medical causes after a medical crisis in their lives.

> It wasn't until I had a son with multiple sclerosis that I realized having money makes it my job to do something. Before my son came along, giving to charity wasn't a big deal. I used to think money didn't have anything to do with whether or not you gave. Now, I know better. If you have money, you are responsible to do something about the state of the world.

> My own problems with my heart got me involved with the heart association. Until I started having troubles, I didn't think having money and giving to charity were related. Now I think that the more you have, the more you should do. Having a major

heart attack really focuses your thinking. I now believe that if you have the money to help people you really should use it to help people. Being rich should mean you are doing something to help people.

While these sentiments are strongest among those Repayers who donate to medical causes, they are also evident among Repayers who contribute to educational institutions.

Before I went to medical school, I would have told you being rich had nothing to do with being morally obligated to give. After medical school, I learned what it means to help someone — and I'm not only talking about patients. I owe the school a hell of a lot. I always said if I made it, I would do something for the school. I made it. So, I always contribute to all the fund-raising drives.

Repayers Give Because Good Results Follow

Repayers share an intimate, almost tangible sense of the results that follow their giving because they have almost all been on the receiving end of the same service. They are so convinced of the good that the act of giving, rather than the motive behind the act, comes to define philanthropy for them. Among Repayers, 81.0 percent define philanthropy by actions instead of motivation. For Repayers, their sense of commitment to the worthy causes they support supersedes issues of motive.

I'm not concerned with semantics. I want results and to get results you got to have money. People give for all sorts of reasons. What difference does it make? If they give they give. There are too many things that have to get done to be concerned with why they give as long as they do. It doesn't matter where the money comes from, it doesn't matter why they do it, it matters what you do with the money they give you.

> Those people who talk about proper moral motivations are pretty naive. Who cares why someone donates as long as they do. The charities I'm involved with need the funds and we can make a difference with every dollar we get. That's what counts.

The point that the result is what is important was clearly made by a major donor and fund raiser to AIDS charities:

> I'd take money from the devil to help victims of AIDS, and I would, in my heart, think of the devil as a philanthropist.

Repayers Give Because Nonprofit Agencies Are More Helpful Than Government Agencies

Nearly all Repayers (92.2%) believe that nonprofits are better positioned than government to meet the needs of society. For many Repayers, this frustration with government programs is often based on personal dealings with governmental agencies which have been difficult.

> I tried getting help from the government for my mother under a program she qualified for. What a mistake. In the end, it was only the medical institute that was able to do anything. So, now I take good care of the institute, and I am pretty critical of the government.

How Repayers Select Nonprofits

Repayers tend to focus their giving on the institution that helped them, but they also insist on the kind of quality and accountability that means effectiveness. Because of their prior familiarity with the target of their giving, they rarely rely on third-party advisors.

Repayers Insist on Effectiveness

As former constituents, Repayers are extremely sensitive about effectiveness of service delivery and operations, and look for that in the nonprofits they support. Most Repayers (81.0%) agree on the importance of insisting on accountability in the form of a proven track record of effectiveness.

> When I decided to completely get involved with some AIDS charities I was confused about which ones to get involved with. I didn't want to be involved with one that wasn't doing much. I made it a point to figure out which one was the best of the bunch and that's the one I'm involved with.

> I give because it means a great deal to me. I'm not going to waste my time and effort. I'm expecting breakthroughs in medical research in my lifetime. I give so I can get—get results. Because of that, I find out about and then support the best research institutions in order to get results.

Quite often, Repayers are able to gauge the effectiveness of a nonprofit on the basis of their own personal experiences. They are apt to generalize about the quality of the nonprofit from their personal dealings with it.

> Deciding to give something to the school was one of the easiest things I ever did. When I think of what that place did for me I'm confident that I'm backing the right horse.

> The best way to tell about anything is to do it. Unfortunately, I had to go through a tremendous amount of pain to learn how good the people at the medical center are. I don't have a second thought about their ability to deliver, or a second thought about the money I give them.

Repayers Seldom Rely on Advisors

Few Repayers (5.0%) rely on outside or professional advice in making their philanthropic decisions. Many know the nonprofit organizations intimately; others tap into the network of other constituents and donors to evaluate effectiveness. Moreover, the Repayer decision is not generally driven by

financial, estate or tax considerations, nor by opinions of a
social or business network. Instead, Repayers prefer to do
their own decision-making, although they can be influenced
by people close to them such as family and friends.

> It was never a question where I wanted to donate. The hospital
> that did such a great job taking care of Maggie, my sister, was
> who I wanted to give to. I didn't have to check them out, or ask
> anyone for advice. I just did it.

> I give to say thank you and I always know who I want to say
> it to. I don't give to save on taxes or just because some financial
> planner told me it was a good way to save on estate taxes. I don't
> give where other people give to necessarily. I give to say thank
> you, and it is just that simple.

The few Repayers who do seek outside assistance
generally keep control over the decision, but employ an advisor to perform the due diligence. The professional advisor,
when used, is there to confirm the viability of the selected
nonprofit and to ensure that no problems arise.

> I knew the general area I wanted to donate to—cancer research
> and programs to help the families of cancer victims because my
> father died of cancer. But I didn't know which organizations
> would be the best ones to give to. I turned to my law firm and
> they provided me with a detailed evaluation of the alternatives—
> which I paid for. But, the money for the report was more than
> worth it. They gave me a lot of choices with recommendations
> and then I got to choose—just the way I like it.

> I was 99.9 percent sure. It was that little nagging voice in my
> ear that made me a little nervous. I just retained my lawyer to
> get rid of that nagging voice. He checked them out and gave
> me a clean bill of health on them. It was worth the extra effort
> not to have any doubts.

What Repayers Look for After the Gift

Repayers generally do not want to be involved on a day-to-day basis, but appreciate confirmation of their assumptions in selecting the nonprofit in the first place. Repayers want to be aware of what is happening and appreciate it when they can contribute more than money.

Repayers Want Nonprofits to Focus on Their Constituents, Not Their Donors

Repayers do not want to be ignored, or discounted. They want to be kept informed; they want to be valued. But they do not want the focus of attention taken off constituents. When 75.3 percent of Repayers say it is very important that the nonprofit have their best interest at heart, they mean the overarching interest that draws donor and nonprofit together. For Repayers to be satisfied, the focus of the nonprofit should be on the beneficiaries of the charities' services and not on donors like themselves.

My interests are the interests of the students. They are one and the same. If my donations help make it possible for the school to serve them well with new programs and great facilities, and I am kept up to date on what is happening, then I feel like I have been served well. I don't want the school to use my money to create new programs for donors.

I give to find a cure for breast cancer. That's all that's important. If the center has best interests at heart, then they will focus their every effort on doing their very best to find a cure. I don't want them to focus any effort on me or other donors.

The hospital should concentrate on cancer patients. That's what they're supposed to do; that's what I'm giving them the money to do. If they didn't concentrate on the patients, why would I want to give them any money? I'm not important, I don't want any recognition or special attention, and I don't think other donors should either. I just want to be kept informed.

Repayers Do Not Want Individual Attention and Recognition from Nonprofits

Repayers and Dynasts are the least interested in the attentions of the nonprofit. Less than one in ten (9.5%) Repayers say individual attention is very important to them.

> I want them to concentrate on helping the children—not to spend time and energy on me. The reason the home exists is for the children, not for the donors.

> The school's mission is to teach and they shouldn't be wasting their time trying to curry favor with me. I'm going to continue giving regardless of how much attention they pay, so we'd all feel better if they continued to focus on the students.

Repayers Want Their Simple, Uncluttered Motives to Be Understood

Compared to other philanthropic personalities, Repayers appear less concerned that the nonprofit understand them and their motives for giving. Less than half of Repayers (42.9%) think it is very important that nonprofits have a detailed knowledge of their motivations for giving. However, follow-up interviews determined that this is because most Repayers believe their motivations are obvious and self-evident.

> It's not critical that the heart association knows why I give. Still, I'd be very surprised if everyone didn't know my father died of a heart attack and that I recently had a heart attack.

> I went to school there; I learned my profession there. I think they all know exactly why I give to the college.

Depending on their personal situation, some Repayers are grateful for sensitive acknowledgments of their personal situation and motives. For many Repayers, especially donors to medical nonprofits, the personal situation is still emotionally charged.

> They say time heals all wounds. Well, for me it's taken a long time and I'm still not healed. I can't tell you how much I appreciate it when there's someone who can understand the pain, who can sometimes provide a shoulder to cry on. The place is full of people — staff and volunteers — who understand the pain because we've all been there.

> I'm not into sympathy. I can handle things. But, sometimes it's nice to let your hair down. Sometimes it's nice to talk to people who can relate and the people at the clinic can relate.

Repayers Have Little Need to Be Involved in Operations of the Nonprofit

Only a third (33.3%) of Repayers would like to have an active role in determining how their funds should be used by the nonprofit. Those who want more involvement typically secure for themselves a seat on the board or on a committee. Repayers who feel they should not be involved say the reason is they are not competent to make such decisions.

> I don't know a thing about the science that goes into researching this disease. I am very happy to stay at arm's length and leave all the decisions about which projects should be funded to the scientists and doctors.

> I know the general direction I want things to go in. That's why I gave my money to this particular group. But, I'm not able to tell anyone what to do or how to do it. I don't have a clue. I just would like to get updates, but stay out of the day-to-day.

Repayers contributing to educational institutions tend to feel the same way. They recognize their limited expertise in the area and generally prefer to leave decisions in the hands of the experts.

> When I want something done I hire a pro and let him call the shots. It's the same with the school I give to. The university people are the pros. I let them call the shots.

On the other hand, those Repayers interested in the operations of the nonprofit explain it as a need to ensure that their funds are used the way they intended them to be used. For these Repayers, the need to obtain results motivates them to take more active roles.

> The programs have to help people. You have to see that they help people. I remember I bounced around between support groups until I found this one. They were able to make me feel that I shouldn't go away and die, that I was a worthy human being. Whenever I give money, I think it is important to get involved enough to see that the place is doing things that matter.

Repayers Do Not Seek Formal Recognition

In general, Repayers believe they have already benefited from the relationship with the nonprofit, and as a result, they do not usually seek the additional recognition, status, connections, or benefits often sought by other donors. Repayers say they find it distasteful that other donors appear to be looking for personal favors, publicity, or honors from a nonprofit institution.

> Frankly, I have a hard time stomaching big shot alumni who seem to only want their egos stroked. If you care about the school you give. I care, so I give. I'm not looking to get anything out of it, and I wish other people wouldn't be looking to get something out of it, either.

> I was put off when they wanted to make a big fuss over my involvement. All the pomp and circumstances they were proposing put me off. I'm giving because it is the right thing to do, and I prefer to be low key about the whole thing.

While it is sort of nice to be honored, the thought of an awards dinner will only bring up bad memories for me. I understand that lots of people like to be honored. Don't get me wrong, I think it's worthwhile if you like that sort of thing. It's just not for me.

Summary

Repayers have had some experience that changed their life, an experience which created in them a feeling of obligation or gratitude. These experiences constellate around educational institutions and medical events, and Repayers focus their giving on these two nonprofit types. Repayers do not seek recognition for themselves; as a general rule, they prefer that nonprofits focus on constituents. They are appreciative when the officers of the nonprofit are sensitive to their reasons for being philanthropic as well as their own personal situation.

7

The Dynast:
Doing Good Is a Family Tradition

As I was growing up, my brother, sister, and I learned it was our responsibility to help those less fortunate. We all still believe that we must help others. Our mother, God rest her soul, would be proud of us.

Giving is just something our family does and has always done. In our family giving is just a natural thing to do.

Who Are Dynasts?

The philanthropic motivation of Dynasts stems from their early childhood socialization. Giving is something their family always stood for, and they believe it is expected of them to support nonprofits. Although Dynasts have been significant figures in philanthropy for some time, they now comprise 8.3 percent of major donors.

Inherited wealth is concentrated in the Dynast segment; 44.1 percent say their source of wealth was an inheritance. For the remainder (56.3%), the source of wealth for philanthropic giving is a family business inherited along with a family tradition of charitable support. Nearly all Dynasts are college educated (93.7%), and there are as many women as men in this segment.

Why Dynasts Give

Dynasts give because philanthropy is a strong family value.

Dynasts Give Because Their Families Have Taught Them It Is Important

For all Dynasts, philanthropy was something learned at home; it was an integral facet of their upbringing. In effect, Dynasts were socialized into the world of philanthropy.

> I never thought about it until I hit college. Charity was always what my family did. We just all grew up with discussions about it, with going to charity affairs, with people interested in issues.

> When I was growing up, I got two allowances. One was for me to spend; one was for me to give to charity. That is how all the kids in my family learned to be charitable.

Popular imagery has it that Dynasts inherited their wealth, and this is often the case. Among these Dynasts, a good proportion (44.1%) did inherit their wealth. But wealth in the family of origin is not a necessary condition for the communication of philanthropic values; some Dynasts come from poorer families that brought up their children with the same tradition of giving.

> Growing up I never had any money. My family was real poor. Still, we always gave to those who had even less. I grew up knowing that no matter how much I had or how much I didn't have, I should always give to the needy.

Dynasts support a wide range of nonprofits and are more likely than the other philanthropic personalities to support nonprofits out of the mainstream. Dynasts more commonly support nonprofits directed at helping the economically disadvantaged, for example. In part, this may be explained by Dynasts' relatively low need for social approval of their actions. It is also a function of generational change among Dynasts. The new generation of heirs lives out the tradition, but in their own way—by supporting causes of their choice. While younger Dynasts continue the family tradition of philanthropy, they often seek to be influential in a new area. They are looking to come out from behind the family shadow and establish themselves as individuals in the nonprofit arena.

> My whole family is heavily into charity, but it's always the same ones—the church, the museum, the big name causes. I wanted to strike out on my own and get hooked up with innovative people who are really focused on today's issues. That's why I go my own way when it comes to picking causes.

> My charity says things about me. I want to do things that are important as I see them. I don't get excited about the stuff my parents and grandparents were interested in, so I support a completely different set of causes than they do.

Dynasts Give Because Philanthropy Is Part of Their Self-Concept

Dynasts have high internal motivation to give. Their rewards—self-identity, conforming to family and class values, and giving itself—are all internal. Dynasts are less externally motivated than Communitarians or Socialites since they do not seek group rewards such as networking or social affairs. As a result, most Dynasts (69.7%) place a greater value on the motivation for giving than on the value of the act itself.

> Giving with ulterior motives like getting new clients or promoting a business isn't really giving in my book. It's more like a disguised business deal and that just isn't philanthropy.

> I grew up with a tradition of giving. You give because it's the right thing to do, not because you are guilty about having money or something like that. If you don't give because it's the right thing to do, well, it's sort of like buying your way in or cheating.

We have to teach what's right and wrong, and giving to give without any expectation of getting is what's right.

A minority of Dynasts feel differently, and think that
it is the ends—the philanthropic acts themselves—and not
the means, that really count.

My great grandfather was one mean bastard—he was totally ruth-
less in running his company and he screwed over anyone who
got in his way. But, you know, people also call him a great humanitarian and philanthropist. He endowed all sorts of schools
and hospitals. I think he did it—from the stories my parents and
some of my other relatives and family friends told me—so he
could be immortal. But, you know, it doesn't make a difference
why. Not one of the schools or hospitals ever questioned him
about how he made the money he gave them. I often question
whether he was a great humanitarian, but I never question if
he was a great philanthropist.

It's just how you want to count it up. I count what people do
and call it charity. The way I figure, if you only gave the name
'charitable' to people who were pure of heart, you would have
a very short list.

Dynasts Give Because They Believe Philanthropy Is Everyone's Responsibility

Although their wealth allows them to be more influential or
effective as donors, Dynasts believe everyone should support
nonprofits, no matter what his or her social position. In growing up in an environment promoting philanthropy, Dynasts
internalized the need to be charitable. They now identify this
behavior as basic to their characters, and to a large extent,
expect it of everyone.

It is the responsibility of everyone to do what they can in terms
of giving to charity. How little or how much depends on what
they can do, but that's not what counts. What counts is the fact
that they're doing what they can.

> I grew up poor and my family was always real charitable. Now that I have money, I'm still real charitable, but I can give more. It doesn't make any difference how much money you have, you should always be charitable.

Dynasts believe individuals should be as charitable as possible, regardless of economic resources.

> Moral responsibility is not determined by your resources, it's determined by your outlook. My parents brought me up right and that means taking responsibility for my life. And, one of the things that means is doing what I can to support worthwhile charities.

> As a child I looked down upon people who were not giving. Now that I am an adult, I understand many things differently, but I can't shake that childhood feeling.

Dynasts Give Because Private Philanthropy Is More Effective Than Government Programs

All Dynasts hold that nonprofits are significantly more capable of meeting the needs of society than the government for several reasons. One reason is because Dynasts tend to focus on, as one of them put it, "cutting edge causes and causes that make a difference." Another reason is their shared belief that government is "bureaucratic and slow when it comes to what really matters—people and our world." Another reason is that they, and the nonprofits they support, can focus on a specific issue.

> A lot of the nonprofits are very much in synch with what's going on. The government tends to react only after people are mobilized and have pushed them to it.

> Nonprofits have their limitations. But nonprofits also are making the right type of effort and they are there to help. The government, and it doesn't matter who's in charge, Republican or Democrat, is just too big to act effectively it seems.

How Dynasts Select Nonprofits

Dynasts are among the most careful of all philanthropic personalities in selecting nonprofits to support. Dynasts are a frequent target of fund raisers and solicitors of all sorts, and they are generally inundated with requests to give. As a result of these pressures, Dynasts take great care in researching and evaluating nonprofits, and are the segment most likely to employ advisors to assist them in the process.

Dynasts Are Careful Before They Commit to Supporting a Nonprofit

All Dynasts believe it is vital to make a personal and detailed evaluation of a nonprofit before making a decision to donate. The objective of this research is to identify nonprofits that make a real difference.

> I've grown up giving to nonprofits. I have come to recognize that some have too much overhead and administration, and others can be inefficient at what they do. I go to a lot of trouble to make sure the charities I give to are doing relevant work and that they are doing it well.

> My father taught me compassion. But he also taught me the value of a dollar. I'll always be compassionate *and* I'll always make sure the dollars I give get value. How I do that is research nonprofits very carefully.

Dynasts want to understand in detail the mission and activities of the nonprofits they are considering. They want to be well informed about the distinctiveness and successes of the nonprofits they choose to support. This concern with day-to-day operations is especially the case where the nonprofit in question is not in the traditional mainstream.

> Before I would do more than write a check for a few hundred dollars, I ask them (the officers of the nonprofit) to explain to

me what they're all about. I want to get to know them in great detail—the ins and outs of their organization. I learned this all from my grandfather.

I had a father who drilled it into me that whatever I do with my money is fine, just so long as I look into it hard. Some of the times my selections don't work out and that even means the charities I have supported. So long as I take a good hard look at who they (the nonprofits) are, what they're trying to do and it all looks good then I made the best decision I could at the time.

Dynasts Are Likely to Employ Professional Advisors to Help Them in Their Giving Decisions

Aside from the financial advisors the affluent employ for strictly financial advice, Dynasts increasingly look to "experts" for philanthropic advice and assistance in the accountability issues discussed above. More specifically, Dynasts seek assistance in making decisions about whom to give to, how to structure the giving program, and when to give. The use of philanthropic advisors was most pronounced among Dynasts. Over half (61.5%) of Dynasts look to advisors to assist them in working through the research, evaluation, and eventual selection decision processes.

In part, these advisors help with the complex financial, estate, and tax consequences of major gifts. These advisors are sometimes used as intermediaries between the donor and the nonprofit. The philanthropic advisor may also negotiate with a nonprofit on the donor's behalf for recognitions and board or committee memberships it would be unseemly to ask for directly.

With all the fund raisers who seek me out, I had to get some qualified help. My family always was heavily involved in charitable causes. I needed to do something that wasn't what my mother or father were doing. I knew I wanted to concentrate on children's causes, but not in the conventional way. It meant I had to find someone to guide me through the "labyrinth of charities."

Arthur, my attorney, has always helped me with family financial issues. Evaluating charity giving is just an extension of the
services his firm provides me. I'm the one making the decision.
He just acts as a great sounding board.

Dynasts who do not use a philanthropic advisor feel
that their upbringing provided them with the expertise to
effectively make giving decisions. As charity has been a part
of their lives, they believe they are more than competent to
deal with these decisions unaided.

I was brought up with philanthropy. My whole family was and
still is into it. I don't need an outsider telling me how to give—I
know how. In our family, we all know how.

I understand the ins and outs of charities. I was taught this first
on my father's knee and then as a trustee of the family's foundation. I, for one, don't need any help in making charitable decisions.

What Dynasts Look for After the Gift

Dynasts expect the nonprofit to continue to operate efficiently and well after the gift, and do not usually look for
a continuing role in overseeing use of the funds. Only when
they feel that the nonprofit is not performing will they want
to get directly involved. Dynasts are not particularly concerned with accolades.

Dynasts Are Touchy on the Issue of Tradition

Most Dynasts feel strongly (81.3%) that nonprofits should
be familiar with their motivations for giving. For all Dynasts,
giving is a tradition. However, for different generations of
Dynasts, tradition takes on different meanings. Dynasts are
pleased when their nonprofit affiliates understand their respect for philanthropic tradition and reinforce it. The older
generation of Dynasts now giving, for example, tends to re-
vere the traditions of previous generations.

For me, giving is a family legacy. I give to some of the same organizations my father did, and that continuity is important to
me. I am very gratified when the organizations I support treat
the memory of my father with respect.

The younger generation of Dynasts, by contrast, sees
philanthropy itself as the tradition, and is more likely to break
with their elders in the type of charities they support.

I wasn't very interested in giving to the same charities my parents supported. I wanted to do something on my own. It was
hard to leave certain charities supported by my parents, but to
me the important thing is the tradition of giving, not the tradition of giving to a particular organization.

At this one nonprofit, they treat me like my mother's son. I'm
28 and I'm my own person as well. One of the reasons I am moving my support to new charities is that I want to be considered
on my own, not just as the new member of the family.

Nonprofits which do not take the time to understand
the subtle motives of the Dynast may erode some of the basis for their support. Dynasts expect to develop an interpersonal as well as professional relationship with key individuals
of the nonprofits they support. Dynasts express a clear desire
to know the people they are involved with and for those people to know them.

It's valuable to be able to relate to the people you're trusting to
use your money wisely. I expect they will want to know about
me, too. I see this as a long term relationship which will work
well only if we know each other well.

My whole family, for generations, has been into philanthropy.
Part of my legacy is philanthropy. Someday, I will run the family foundation. I like it when fund raisers realize I'm not an extension of my parents, and go to the trouble of understanding
me and communicating that understanding to me. That's empathy, and I am likely to reward empathy with funding, foundation support, and my contacts.

Dynasts Do Expect Nonprofits to Be Consistent in Recollecting the Motivations and Rationale for the Gift

Having gone through a lengthy selection process, Dynasts expect their nonprofits to stay the course. They expect non-profits will remember the gift by continuing to operate in ways consistent with the spirit of the gift and the donor, by being attentive to donors, and by keeping them informed and involved.

> My parents taught me the value of charity. They also taught me that the better charities will also be very concerned about my welfare. Not just because I give them money, but because that's what charity is about.

> For generations our whole family gave, and we give away lots of money today. When we were small, my brother and sisters and I were given money and we learned how to give it to charity. Even as kids, we only gave it to the people in charge of the charities who treated us well as people. I learned that lesson well. So, that's what I do today.

Dynasts Expect Nonprofits to Stay Focused on Their Missions Instead of Catering to Major Donors

Of all segments, Dynasts are the least interested in nonprofits being attentive to them. Only 6.3 percent of Dynasts believe that individual attention directed at donors is very important. Instead, Dynasts want the nonprofits they support to stay focused on their core mission, rather than divert resources to the care of donors.

> Growing up charitable, I grew to understand that giving is to truly benefit others. The benefits I receive are from the act of giving, not from anything the charity could do for me. I feel let down if they (the officers of the nonprofit) concentrated on me and not on those people who really need their attention.

I want them to understand me and at the very same time I don't want the effort they make with me to distract them from what they're about. It sounds a little paradoxical but it really isn't. It is not difficult to be sensitive to me and direct the bulk of their energies at doing a good job for the disadvantaged.

Most Dynasts Defer to a Well-Managed Nonprofit in Day-to-Day Decisions; Only a Few Want Involvement

Relatively few Dynasts (31.3%) believe they should take an active role in determining how their gifts should be utilized. Overall, Dynasts believe nonprofit professionals are well suited to make decisions regarding the nature of programs promoted by the nonprofits. Their confidence in the managers of the nonprofit is a function of their painstaking selection process.

When I pick which charities to give to, I take a lot of time. I am sure I understand their objectives and processes. I am especially sure I come to have confidence in their professionals and executives. Then, I give and try to not get in their way.

I have seen too many donors interfere with good charities by trying to tell them how to do their job. It's like going to a rodeo and not be on the card, but jumping in anyway. If donors want to help they should get on committees. Otherwise, they should move on. I make my choice, and put my money down.

Dynasts who are interested in being involved in the managerial aspects of the nonprofit generally arrange to join the board or committees which interest them. Some Dynasts believe that commitment to a nonprofit means giving of time as well as money.

I was taught to get involved—me, personally. It isn't enough just to give. I see it as my responsibility to give them assistance when I think it could help.

As I was growing up—and this goes for my whole family—I came to understand how important it is to be present and involved when important decisions are being made. I think it is foolish to think that you can give away large sums of money and walk away. You have to be around to make sure it's used properly, just the way you should watch over any investment. I don't want to command or dominate. I only want to be involved when I can help.

Dynasts want to do creative charitable work and are not specifically interested in being honored for behavior they see as essential. Because their philanthropic behavior was acquired early in life, it feels natural and is not viewed as something which merits special recognition.

I'm not doing this for the glory or to see my name in lights or so that everybody will say nice things about me. It's because I care, deep down care. My brothers and sisters and I would talk about it. None of us are interested in the awards. Our award is knowing that we've done something that counted.

I don't like it when they suggest the idea of giving me an award or a dinner in my name. It makes me feel that it's not about doing good. I think it confuses the act of charity with the personal benefits of charity. I grew up with charity and my father was always embarrassed by all the fuss. I guess I'm the same way.

Summary

Many Dynasts represent the old monied class where giving is a tradition and philanthropy is an important part of socialization in the family. Increasingly, Dynasts of the new generation show signs of going their own ways, not breaking with the tradition of giving, but with the type of nonprofits supported. Dynasts have a more diverse giving portfolio than any other segment. They are methodical in selecting nonprofits to support and often use professional advisors in the process. Once having selected, however, Dynasts usually prefer a role in the wings, expecting only that the nonprofit continue to perform excellently on their behalf.

Part Two

CULTIVATING MAJOR DONORS
WITH THE
SEVEN FACES FRAMEWORK

Effective fund raising is based on understanding donor's motivations and goals. Helping fund raisers understand donors, especially affluent individual donors, is what the Philanthropic Personality approach provides.

Understanding, of course, is not enough. Fund raisers have to move from understanding to action. In addition to a detailed familiarity with each of the Seven Faces of Philanthropy, fund raisers need to know how to develop a coherent strategy for working with that framework. In the first place, they must know how to find and attract prospective donors of the various types, then they must be able to motivate those individuals to support a particular nonprofit. Since raising money is the critical success factor, it is imperative that fund raisers properly position the various giving strategies against the needs of each Philanthropic Personality. Finally, it is absolutely necessary to empower the philanthropist. This last step is ongoing, and when well done, we find that fund raisers empower philanthropists in all aspects of the continuing relationship between nonprofit and major donor.

Chapter Eight explores how fund raisers can take full advantage of existing charity networks. The key to identifying and developing affluent individuals into prospective donors is referrals made through the charity network. There are several ways of working through charity networks, each specific to Philanthropic Personality. One is by capitalizing on the relationships the nonprofit has with current major donors; another is by accessing intermediary channels composed of the legal, financial, and philanthropic advisors to the affluent.

Chapter Nine describes how fund raisers can craft a vision which will effectively link the nonprofit to the benefits sought by each Philanthropic Personality. The process of crafting the vision includes three phases. First, the fund raiser must identify the Philanthropic Personality of the affluent prospect. This chapter provides a framework that will enable fund raisers to recognize each of the seven Philanthropic Personalities in an unobtrusive way. Once the Philanthropic Personality has been established, the next phase is to create a bond between the nonprofit and the wealthy individual by using descriptive language especially meaningful to each donor type. The final phase of this process is to validate the philanthropist's commitment to the nonprofit by creating opportunity for them to hear personal testimonials from donors of the same Philanthropic Personality who are already involved with the nonprofit.

Chapter Ten takes up the issue of charitable giving strategies. A wide array of strategies is available to the affluent — various types of trusts, donor-advised funds, foundations, gift annuities, and the like. Each Philanthropic Personality has a different profile when it comes to preferences for giving strategies, and fund raisers will find these preferences useful in their development planning.

Finally, Chapter Eleven discusses strategies fund raisers and other nonprofit executives can use to empower the philanthropist. To ensure long-term support for the nonprofit, it is vital that wealthy philanthropists feel psychologically involved with the nonprofit. The most effective involvement is achieved through personal participation. Since each Philanthropic Personality prefers to be involved and to participate in a different way, just how fund raisers can empower philanthropists to become involved in ways consistent with their Philanthropic Personality is discussed in the chapter.

This entire process is shown schematically below and is explained in detail in the next four chapters.

Implementing the Seven Faces Framework

Step 1. Leveraging the Charity Network
- Capitalize on existing networks with major donors
- Tap into various charity networks
- Develop intermediary channels

Step 2. Crafting the Vision
- Identify the prospective donor's philanthropic personality
- Create empathy by using meaningful language
- Utilize appropriate testimonials

Step 3. Promoting Charitable Giving Strategies
- Educate philanthropists to the various giving strategies
- Emphasize charitable remainder trusts and private foundations
- Establish a program of strategic alliances with advisors to the affluent

Step 4. Empowering the Philanthropist
- Encourage participation in interacting with major donors
- Empower philanthropists through involvement
- Strengthen the relationship through promotion and intermediaries

8

Making Connections Through Charity Networks

It's not what you know, but who you know. It's just good business to use connections to get things done. Any fund raiser worth his salt will get the rich guys already at the charity to bring in their friends. It sounds like a cliché, but rich people know rich people, that's just the way it is.

—*An Investor*

The world runs on connections. And, connections are what make the nonprofits run. Someone with money and clout is the perfect person to introduce someone else with money and clout to the senior staff of a charity. It just works that way.

—*A Dynast*

The first step in cultivating wealthy donors is attracting them to a particular nonprofit. Experienced fund raisers know that all efforts in attracting the wealthy are built on a web of connections between a prospective donor and a charitable organization. By understanding what the potential connections are and by understanding how this process operates, fund-raising executives create effective and lasting relationships with affluent prospects. As this chapter will demonstrate, the single most effective set of connections

111

between donor prospect and nonprofit lies in the charity network.

Understanding Charity Networks

Social influence theory explains that one of the means by which people identify the correct course of action is to talk with others and find out how they behave (Cialdini, 1984). For fund raisers seeking to positively influence behavior, understanding the dynamics of word-of-mouth is crucial, as donors who are considering a decision as major as the creation of a foundation or trust will seek out others and obtain their opinion. Investors, for example, who seek to create a charitable remainder trust will perceive this as a complex and risky task with adverse and severe tax consequences if not properly executed. These Investors will seek out people they know who have previously established such a trust for advice. Equally, a Communitarian who would like to expand his business and social networks will find other business owners with charitable connections and ask for their advice and input. The very active peer groups of Socialites have already been described. Because most donors perceive the philanthropic task as complex and somewhat risky, most rely to a greater or lesser degree on word-of-mouth testimonials from others to identify, screen, and select a nonprofit (the extent of this activity is shown in Figure 8.1). While Socialites are the group most influenced by information obtained from their referral networks, and Altruists the least, all donors except Repayers say they depend on others' opinions in making their decisions.

Research on word-of-mouth has provided several findings of particular relevance to fund raisers interested in leveraging the system. Most important is that credibility of word-of-mouth is enhanced under two conditions: the source of information is similar to the one seeking input, and the source is of higher or desirable status.

> When I saw all those famous people at the gala, I knew this charity was a class act. It helped me decide to get more involved with them.
> — A *Socialite*

Figure 8.1. Importance of Charity Networks.

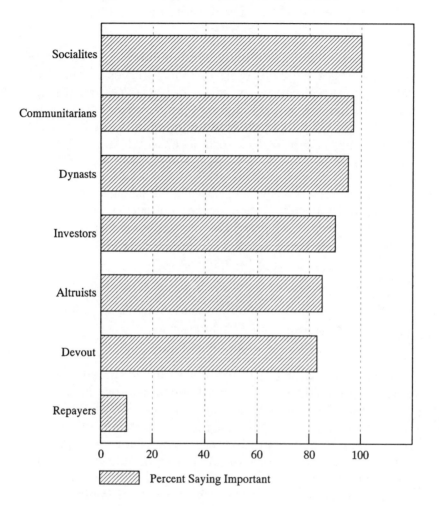

I have a lot of respect for some of the leaders in this city. A big helper in my decision to also join was when I found out they were part of the children's education group.

—*A Communitarian*

I felt I owed the college something, but I wasn't quite sure until I saw someone who was already a member of the President's

Club. If Bob thought it was a good place to put his money, I
felt confident that it was a good place to put mine.
        —A *Repayer*

Moreover, word-of-mouth also plays a significant role
after a decision is made. Word-of-mouth serves as a form of
post-decision validation for many donors. Wealthy philanthropists, like anyone else, like to feel they made correct decisions, especially when their reputation is involved, and will
be especially receptive to information which supports their
decisions once they have been made (Festinger, 1969).

I know what I want to do, so I looked into things and made my
decision. I was pretty pleased to find out later who else was
involved—several people I had heard of but never met. Finding
that out made me feel good about my decision.
        —A *Communitarian*

I've gone and made up my mind. Still, when you see who else
is there it gives me a good feeling all over that I'm in with people who are going to really try to make a difference.
        —An *Investor*

As it turns out, the wealthy are primarily directed to specific nonprofits through the charity networks specific to their
personality. Charity networks are composed of all the interlocking relationships supporting nonprofits: donors, their advisors, and other nonprofits. In repeated interviews with philanthropists, the importance and dynamics of charity networks
were confirmed. From the perspective of the philanthropic
personalities, charity networks include the social affinity groups
composed of donors and prospective donors. They are the de-
terminant influencers of ultimate choice of nonprofits for
major donors. While philanthropists say they personally make
the final decision, 56.2 percent of affluent donors rated the
recommendations of others as critical in the process.

I have to add up all the different pieces of advice I get. I go get
tons of advice from my friends and even the friends of my friends.
        —A *Socialite*

I synthesize what I learn to form my opinion and decision about charities. I get the best information to be synthesized from other well-established and respected citizens.

— A *Communitarian*

I take a lot of time and I rely on the input of a great many people in forming my assessment. I can't imagine doing it any other way.

— An *Altruist*

Structurally, these charity networks resemble word-of-mouth–based referral systems typical of service settings which are hard for consumers to evaluate (Prince, 1991). Referral networks are defined as social networks which evolve for the two-way flow of information about the purchasing of goods and services (Reingen and Kernan, 1986). Referral networks are an aspect of word-of-mouth exchanges among consumers of a service.

Word-of-mouth has been repeatedly shown to have a major effect on the types of purchase decisions most similar to the choice decision of a major donor for nonprofit (Richins, 1983; Herr and others, 1991; File and Prince, 1992). The findings of this research on philanthropists extends the exploration of word-of-mouth and referral networks to consideration of their role, importance, and implications in nonprofit settings. Because of the distinctive dynamics of nonprofits, referral networks in this context will be referred to as charity networks.

Charity networks provide philanthropists with factual information about organizations, aid them in managing their expectations about the benefits of involvement, and enable donors to avoid certain kinds of risk. For affluent individual donors, aspects of the decision to support a nonprofit in a significant way resemble other decisions such as investments or the transfer of any significant sum of money. Most donors are aware that various pitfalls exist and they are motivated to avoid as many as they can. As a result, major donors need considerable information in making giving decisions, depending on the philanthropic personality. The degree and nature of perceived risk varies with philanthropic personality. For Communitarians, the risk may be loss of time and business opportunity should they become involved with a nonprofit that does not meet their needs of business networking as well as their desire to do good. Or, the risk may be public association with a nonprofit that does an inadequate or controversial job in tackling local issues. For Socialites, the risk is in becoming overly involved with nonprofits their social group will not also support with voluntary actions, donations, and participation at fund raisers. For the Devout, the risk is in choosing a nonprofit out of keeping with the values of their religious group. For Investors, the risk is in giving to a poorly managed organization so the leverage of the gift appears wasted, and so on.

To improve their information flow and avoid the risks common to donors of their philanthropic personality, donors rely on charity networks to help them effectively screen and select nonprofits to become affiliated with. Reliable information of the type philanthropists need to reduce their perceived risk is generally unavailable from formal information channels such as the nonprofit itself. Because philanthropists are at a considerable information disadvantage, they compensate by tapping their charity network.

In recent years, the trend is for these informal referral networks to be increasingly supplemented by formal intermediaries, philanthropic advisors, although these are not widespread as yet. Philanthropic advisors are used when it appears that their intervention can increase the probability of a successful donor-nonprofit relationship. In addition, financial and legal advisors are often instrumental in assisting wealthy donors in their philanthropy.

The existence of charitable networks and the rise of philanthropic advisors makes fund raising from the affluent more challenging for nonprofits. Because donors obtain so much information from the charity networks, they rely less on information directly from nonprofits.

In sum, information about charitable organizations is communicated from person to person in loosely coupled social systems called here charity networks. The word-of-mouth, both positive and negative, communicated through the charity networks characteristic of each philanthropic personality type is the way the affluent reach decisions about becoming affiliated with specific nonprofits.

Philanthropic Personality Specific to Charity Networks

Six of the seven philanthropic personalities rely heavily on charity networks. However, the nature, membership, and dynamics of the charity network are different for each philanthropic personality as is shown in Table 8.1 and discussed in the following sections.

Table 8.1. Philanthropic Personality and
Specific Charitable Networks.

Philanthropic personality	Use of charitable network
Repayers	The exception: selection of nonprofit based on own experience as beneficiary
Communitarians	Rely on charity networks made up of other business owners; overlaps with other affiliations—for example, Rotary
Socialites	Charity network is all important; virtually a group, not an individual, decision
Altruists	Small charity network made up of close friends and family
Devout	Charity network overlaps with religious community
Investors	Qualify nonprofits through business contacts
Dynasts	Reject charity network of parents and develop their own among friends of their generation

Note that Repayers are the exception to the general tendency of donors to be dependent on charity networks. In contrast to other philanthropic personalities, Repayers base their decision on their individual experiences as beneficiaries and not on a social network.

Of All Donor Types, Repayers Rely on Charity Networks the Least

For Repayers, their direct, personal experience as a beneficiary of a nonprofit institution subsequently serves as the basis for their decision to become involved with the same organization. Almost all (95.2%) Repayers say that their own research was the basis for their decision to create a different relationship with nonprofit, that of donor.

> When it's all said and done, if it isn't right, I never want to be cross with anyone but myself. On my charity decisions, I don't ask anyone else's opinion. I'm a big boy. I can make the decision myself so long as I take the time and examine all the alternatives.

> Most all my life I was brittle. My illness was like a trip into the heart of the fire — it made me hard. Now, I call the shots and make all the decisions. I make sure I look at the situation with the medical center and the research organizations, I try to ask the right questions and I make the best decision I can based on my own research and feelings. I don't talk it over with many people.

Repayers do their research directly with nonprofits. A very high proportion of Repayers (95.2%) had a pre-existing relationship with the nonprofit beneficiary of their major gift, and this relationship facilitates information flow.

> I decided to get involved with the hospital because of my condition. I got to know a lot of people while I was in the hospital, and I got to know a lot about the hospital itself. The decision to support them was a very personal decision, but it wasn't a hard one since I knew them so well.

> You have to understand where I'm coming from. My life was changed because of the place. I don't mean a little bit changed, I mean drastically changed — mongo bongo changed. I still kept in touch with some people there, and when it became possible

for me to help them out, I knew who to call. Where else would I donate money? Let's get real.

Repayers emphasize the personal relationship they have with staff members of the nonprofit. This interpersonal factor is very important to almost all (95.2%) Repayers. Because Repayers become involved in many ways with the nonprofits they support, it is important to them to feel they can operate effectively with the staff.

I remember all the pain I felt, the hopelessness. The night nurse. was there to hold my hand. She believed I'd make it, and after a while she made me believe I would make it. She did this for everyone on her floor. An honest-to-goodness nowadays Joan of Arc. She was the reason I got involved with the hospital once I went into remission.

Meaningful interpersonal contact as a stimulus to giving is particularly evident among Repayers who are major benefactors of their educational institutions.

Some of the professors are the reason I made it. Dr. Barkley was so special. He was like a mentor to me. I endowed a chair because I want to make sure he can do for the new students what he did for me.

When someone makes a life-deciding effect on your life, you never forget it and you always want to show you appreciated it. That's the way it was with me and Dr. Thomas. I took every class he ever gave and specialized in his field. I just gave a laboratory in his name to the medical school.

Relatively few (9.5%) Repayers are influenced by a charity network. Those who do rely on a charity network say they do so because the people in it provide personal support systems that help the Repayers make a commitment to the nonprofit.

Other Business Owners Constitute the Charity Network of Communitarians

Almost all Communitarians (96.7%) say that the influence of other business owners is very important to them in making decisions to support nonprofits. Communitarians are themselves business owners who seek, as a major benefit of association with a nonprofit, the opportunity to interact with other business owners in an informal setting. To achieve this objective, they tend to rely on other business owners, with whom they interact in a charity network, for input and advice.

> We are all members of the Rotary Club and we share our experiences and what we hear about most everything and everybody. We spend most of the time talking about money, how to make it, how to invest it, and how to spend it. Under the category of spend we talk about charity giving. I trust these guys and I got hooked up with the charities I did because of the things they said about them and because many of them were also involved.

> I got involved with the rehabilitation unit because Rob got me going to a few of the meetings where I met other people who I happened to know already. Rob and the other guys all own companies just like I do, and if we weren't so much alike I bet I wouldn't have accepted his invitation to see the unit in the first place.

Communitarians are also motivated to act by their personal relationships with the local nonprofit community, although to a lesser extent. About a quarter (22.2%) say their familiarity with the officers of the nonprofit or the work of the organization was a significant factor in their first affiliations.

> I know my community. I've lived here all my life. I know the different charities and who's doing what. I know what I want to do so I just pick out who is doing that and I donate. It's really very simple.

The Input of Their Charity Network Is the Determining Factor for Socialites

All (100%) Socialites said the information they obtained from their charity network was the critical factor in their choice of nonprofits to support. The philanthropic behaviors of Socialites are motivated by their social milieu, and there is some evidence that Socialites make giving decisions only after they are assured that they will get group approval. For Socialites, their charity network consists of other Socialites, people as focused as they are on the philanthropic and social aspects of the fund-raising event.

> I decided to be a leading supporter of the fine arts center, including the museum where there is a room named after me, because my friends and I thought we should all help keep the arts alive. We got together and thought of different ways to spread culture. This was one of them. A scholarship program for financially disadvantaged aspiring talented artists is another. I have to tell you, my friends and I, we work out these things together.

> A friend got me over to the Historical Society and showed me around. She had me speak with the President, and I went back a few times. I talked it over with some other friends, and a couple of months later, I was in charge of an event. It just clicked for me.

Most Socialites explain that their personal discrimination, experience, and research impacts on their initial decision; 52.2 percent said this factor was very important. However, Socialites are inclined to depend on their charity network of social affiliations to provide the information they need to evaluate a nonprofit organization and to determine the social consequences of making an affiliation.

> When I think about getting behind a charity, I rely on family and my hell or high water friends to help me figure it out. They are great sounding boards for all the ideas I have. They help me

with suggestions. I will make the choice, but they help me think
it through.

A Few Intimate Friends and Close Family Members Make Up the Altruists' Charity Network

Most Altruists (85.0%) weigh the suggestions of close friends
and family heavily in making their first connections to nonprofits. Unlike Socialites, Altruists do not have a wide social
network; and unlike Communitarians, they are not as tied
in to the local business community. Altruists rely on a smaller
circle of personal supporters; their charity networks are made
up of close family members and friends.

> I didn't have the slightest idea which charity to become com-
> mitted to. I thought about it a lot and I ended up soliciting sug-
> gestions from a few people whose opinions I place some value
> in. And, they happen to be close family and friends. Actually,
> it was my Aunt who suggested the charity I'm now honorary
> Chairperson at. It's the one I give most of my donations to.

> There's just no way you or I are going to know all of what is
> available charity-wise. That's when it helps to get suggestions
> from other people who think like you do. There are no better
> people for this than close friends and family—no better.

Most Altruists (75.0%) also emphasize their own research and experience in their initial decision to support a
charitable organization. While others might point them in
a particular direction as well as provide valuable information,
Altruists are inclined to personally evaluate all they can find
out about the charity and then decide.

> There were people giving me ideas and that helped my think-
> ing on the matter plenty. But, when the tire met the road, I had
> to take a good look at what was there and make a move.

> My friend Betty kept pushing me to give and get involved. I trust
> Betty, and I did give and get involved, but I had to look at it

all closely and talk with the executives and other people on the staff before I would make a major commitment.

For the Devout, the Charity Network Overlaps with Their Religious Community

Among the Devout, 84.4 percent rated the input from members of their religious community as very influential in the initial process of selecting nonprofits to support. As the charities they typically support often have strong religious affiliations, they seek the advice and counsel of people who share the same religious values.

> In Bible class you can get a good read on who understands God's teachings. I have found these fellow parishioners to be the best place to get the truth about different worthy causes. They all are active in many charities and I believe in their judgment.

> The Rabbi has introduced me to other people who are active in giving and to some good charities. I now give to the Temple and I work with these charities.

To a lesser degree, the Devout say the recommendations of business associates are important in their initial decision on a nonprofit (44.4%). In this way, a few of the Devout resemble Investors and Communitarians. They differ, however, in a second criterion: whether these associates share the same religious convictions.

> I trust what Jacob says when it comes to philanthropy. He is deeply compassionate. He and I are in the same business — diamonds. He is a very wise businessman. Plus, his ideas on philanthropy are right out of the holy book, just like mine are.

> When it comes to charity and who to help I listen to other business owners, but they have to be from the same religion. It's not like I'm a snob. It's not just the same religion; it has to be a very pious person — someone who embraces the teachings of our Lord like I do.

Investors Rely on Their Charity Network to Qualify a Nonprofit

Because Investors emphasize avoiding risk and professionalism in operations, they are careful to obtain considerable data from their charity network about nonprofits before making decisions to become personally involved or to give significant sums. Unlike many of the other personalities, Investors rely on third-party and independent sources of information rather than the more informal personal word-of-mouth information valued by most other segments. Investors are especially reliant (93.5%) on their own research and experience in conducting these evaluations.

> I have to know what the guys running the show are going to do with my money. I want to think they are capable. I have got to feel that they have integrity also. I'm willing to put in the time and spend the money in order to make sure I'm making the right choice, so I speak with people, I contact the Better Business Bureau and anyone else in a position to know. I put a lot of faith in site visits. I made a lot of money because I can read people and make decisions carefully.

> I get a sense of urgency, of wanting to help, whenever I look at a nonprofit. But I have to hold back. In deciding on which nonprofit to support, even on which nonprofit to "make contact" with, I weigh everything. I put all the assets and liabilities of it on a mental balance sheet. I have to take this approach. It's the only one that is logical for me.

Like Communitarians, Investors are also likely to seek out the opinions of fellow business owners in their search for information about charitable organizations; 90.3 percent of Investors are significantly influenced by other business owners who tend to share their bottom line attitude.

> I don't have the time to sift through all that's out there. I talk to some guys I know from the club, who I know are on the ball.

They tell me what they like, and I get them to tell me why and that's more important than who. Asking somebody you think is smart and well connected is a much better way to settle on a charity for me.

I like to talk to people who have the same rational, no-nonsense approach to doing things that I have. I talk to them about business and suppliers and, of course, customers. I also talk to them about charitable giving and charities.

Dynasts Are Embedded in Charity Networks, But Those Networks Change Between the Generations

The input of friends and family are important to Dynasts thinking about supporting nonprofits. Almost all (93.3%) Dynasts rated this factor as very important. However, while the family imparts the tradition of giving, friends seem to provide the more important linkage to specific nonprofits.

I want to do something that's me. My friends understand what I'm into, what causes and issues are important to me personally. They're also involved with charities and they give me suggestions. For example, I got into the whole environmental movement because of Jamie. She helped me understand its importance, she introduced me to some of the people who are doing things, and now I am in it with her.

When I decided to help I had to pick a cause. At that time, I didn't know very much about any of the choices I had. I asked my friends for suggestions and they also acted as sounding boards for me to bounce my ideas off of. They helped me when I finally made a decision.

Implications

For almost all philanthropic personalities, charity networks play a significant role in awareness, screening, evaluation, and selection of nonprofits. When the charity network is tapped, both the valence (the positivity or negativity of the comments) and voice (how intense the comments are) are given significant weight by prospective donors working through a decision process. Once involved with nonprofits, donors usually provide advice and counsel to prospective donors.

The existence of these charity networks offers an opportunity for nonprofits to identify and make meaningful contact with potential donors as part of a relationship development program. This program should include the following steps:

Leverage Existing Relationships with Current Major Donors

Current donors provide the best access to the charity networks and can be persuaded to influence these networks on behalf of the nonprofit. Some philanthropic personalities, such as Socialites and Communitarians, are by nature quite motivated to persuade their friends, family, and associates to help support the nonprofit. The opportunity is particularly attractive, since this research shows that most major donors have never been asked to contact prospective donors on behalf of the nonprofits they support.

- Identify and profile philanthropic personalities of current major donors and identify charity networks that could be tapped. This research has established that other affluent prospects can be identified within the charity networks of current supporters; these include business associates, friends, and other family members.
- Frame the initial appeal from the philanthropic personality of the referring donor. People identified and referred by donors tend to be of the same philanthropic personality type and to share motivations. Thus, fund raisers should talk about referrals in the context of the philanthropic personality. For instance, for Altruists, a request for referrals should suggest close friends and family of the major donor, for Socialites, other charity fund raisers, and

for Communitarians, other business owners and civic leaders.

Emphasize Program Quality and Donor Satisfaction

This can be achieved in several ways.

- Strive to satisfy current donors. Satisfying current donors is critical, because dissatisfied donors are highly likely to spread negative word-of-mouth on the charity network and to discourage other prospective donors.
- Undertake a program of asking donors for regular feedback on how they view relationships with the nonprofit and how satisfied they are.
- Create a response management program to act on all negative feedback received. Experience with affluent individuals in other settings indicates that it is possible to turn dissatisfied people into loyalists again if the response to a complaint is appropriate and thorough. Given the high costs of new donor development, even extreme efforts to protect the donor base are usually worthwhile.

9

Building Relationships with the
Seven Philanthropic Personalities

I get approached all the time, but the charities I respond to are
those that ask a lot of questions about what I'm interested in
and then they tell me just how they could fit into that.
— *A Repayer*

You know what got me interested in that last charity? They sent
someone I know to talk to me who was able to explain what the
charity was about in ways that made perfect sense to me.
— *An Altruist*

Making contact with a wealthy potential donor through the
various charity networks is only the beginning of the development process. That prospective donor now has to be educated about and encouraged to support the nonprofit. Bring-
ing about this level of awareness, education, and commitment
takes skill and time, but the rewards are significant. A donor
who is guided through the process by an expert development
officer translates newfound commitment into current and
planned giving, charitable recruiting, volunteering, and the
provisioning of needed services.

We call this second phase in developing the relationship between a nonprofit and a prospective wealthy donor

128

"Crafting the Vision." In this pivotal phase, fund raisers can successfully create a positive vision of the charitable organization in the mind of the wealthy prospect. When done well, this vision is so compelling that the prospective donor wants to act on behalf of the nonprofit. Fund raisers assist donors in imagining relationships with nonprofits by helping donors realize and acknowledge their principal motivations for giving—their Philanthropic Personality—and showing donors the close fit between their personality and the nonprofit. Creating a long-term relationship between donor and nonprofit begins with this phase. To the extent fund raisers enable wealthy prospects to link their needs, their Philanthropic Personality, to the mission of the nonprofit, a system of long-term mutual support can be nurtured between donors and nonprofits.

Extensive studies of fund raising show that this delicate process of "Crafting the Vision" has three steps. In the first phase, expert development officers say they come to understand the motivations and giving history of a prospective major donor, the needs bracketed in this book as the seven faces. In the second phase, astute fund raisers show donors the ways the mission and activities of a nonprofit dovetail with the interests of the donor. In the third phase, fund raisers help donors become affirmed in their motivations, and in the solid achievements of the nonprofit, by endorsements and testimonials from people known to the donor. The first phase is a crucial one, yet inexperienced fund raisers often make the error of skipping it. In their enthusiasm, they may jump to the second phase, discussing the good works and effectiveness of a nonprofit, rather than spending enough time coming to know the motivations, interests, needs, and wants of a donor. More seasoned fund raisers develop personal systems of coming to know individual donors intimately, and the seven faces framework can be used in this way. That is, the seven faces framework can be used as a "checklist," or second perspective, in deciding whether enough is known about a prospect to begin the next phase in the relationship development process. In such a way, fund raisers can combine their personal process of coming to understand the nature of different donor types with the standard framework of seven faces philanthropic personalities. The process of philanthropic personality identification is crucial as it enables fund raisers to cast the nonprofit in the best light and identify as many points of relationship as possible. For example, seasoned university development officers do not promote new undergraduate dormitories to a prospective donor who graduated from the medical school. Instead, they emphasize the new genetics research lab, or the anatomy lecture hall refurbishment, or the pathology equipment that is needed. This sensitive, second stage of the "Crafting the Vision" process can be thought of as the "Velcro" stage, where as many points of connection between donor and nonprofit as possible are identified and tested. In creating effective communications and connections between people, the use of specific words is important. Experienced fund raisers have developed the art of talking the language of the philanthropist. They communicate in ways that show in-depth understanding of donor interests and that bridge those interests with the nonprofit. By communicating in this way and incorporating the orientations of the philanthropic personalities (as explained in the next section of this chapter), fund raisers can position a nonprofit in the manner most appealing and interesting to specific donors.

Years of fund-raising experience has shown that implementing these first two steps of identification and skilled communication does not guarantee success in getting donors to support the nonprofit. In many cases, especially for the social philanthropic personalities such as Communitarians and Socialites, testimonials from other respected donors are necessary to reinforce and build long-term commitment. Testimonials are highly effective in dispelling the last doubts of wealthy prospects and in validating the fund raiser.

Each of the three steps involved in "Crafting the Vision" is documented and detailed in the following sections.

Phase 1: Identifying Philanthropic Personalities

There is no substitute for research and conversation in this first phase. Background research can and should be conducted on prospective wealthy donors before they are met with formally, and the many ways to do this are described in most books on fund raising. Armed with background information, the best fund raisers engage prospective donors in conversation about their background, current situation, and giving interests, all the time seeking to understand the donor in detail. By gaining familiarity with the underlying motivations of each philanthropic personality through conversation, fund raisers will learn what benefits are sought by prospective affluent donors and be able to identify each donor's philanthropic personality within the seven faces framework.

Expert fund raisers have their own tried-and-true processes for identifying and understanding individual donors' needs. For them, the seven faces framework can be used as a check on their perceptions, as another point of view or confirmation. For those developing major donor fund-raising skills, the seven faces framework can be a useful tool in evolving a personal approach. Using the seven faces framework requires some study on the part of fund raisers due to the detail on the characteristics, motives, and aspects of each philanthropic personality, as explained in previous chapters. Fund raisers and financial advisors who have worked with the seven faces approach say they felt initial uncertainty about their ability to distinguish donors by philanthropic personality, but with experience and quick reference back to materials like the ones in this book, their uncertainties vanished.

Based on this feedback from professional fund raisers applying the methods, and the results of extensive interviewing and focus-group sessions, a methodology for identifying the seven faces philanthropic personality of a wealthy individual was developed. This approach is predicated on evaluating the relative importance and impact of different "life domains" on a potential philanthropist.

By conducting a conversation or series of conversations with a prospective major donor about his or her various "life domains," fund raisers can generate a great deal of information. The "life domains" approach also fits comfortably into the patterns of conversation between people getting to know each other well and is efficient because it is semi-structured.

Its goal is to recognize which of several life domains are of singular importance to any given wealthy individual. Once the dominant life domain or domains are identified, a fund raiser can readily determine which philanthropic personality the donor may fit into and confirm this with follow-up questions.

There are four relevant life domains, which can be quickly recalled as the four "F's": *Family* history, *Financial* orientation, *Fundamental* beliefs, and *Friends* and associates. While some seven faces philanthropic personalities will express the importance of more than one life domain, use of this framework has shown that most emphasize one. By asking an affluent individual questions about each life domain, a fund raiser will be able to readily ascertain the appropriate seven faces philanthropic personality.

The process of identifying the seven faces philanthropic personality through the life domains strategy is straightforward. While getting to know the prospective donor better, a fund raiser brings the conversation around to each different life domain in turn. Based on the response from the wealthy individual, a fund raiser can work through all four life domains to determine the background, interests, and motivations of the affluent person.

When dealing with the life domain concerning *Family* history, fund raisers are on the alert for two factors. Each factor identifies a separate seven faces philanthropic personality. One factor is whether there is a strong tradition of giving within the family, with such hallmarks as family trusts and foundations, early exposure to nonprofits and, often, inherited wealth. If there is, and if this is the only strongly noted issue, then the donor philanthropist is a Dynast.

The other *Family* history factor fund raisers should look for is significant situational change over the course of the affluent individual's life such as changes in social class due to education or a severe medical event affecting the donor personally. If such a significant event is found and is the most strongly noted issue, then the philanthropist is a Repayer. Repayers are among the easiest donor types to identify.

When exploring the life domain of *Financial* orientation, the key issue is the extent to which the affluent individual utilizes a monetary calculus in making philanthropic decisions. That is, is the donor particularly concerned with personal tax and estate planning issues, or interested in "businesslike" performance statistics about the nonprofit. The Investor will stand out with respect to this issue.

The life domain of *Fundamental* beliefs is where fund raisers identify both the Altruist and the Devout as well as distinguish between them. Both these philanthropic personalities hold well thought-out values and make an effort to conform their lives to higher principles. If prospective donors speak about living a moral life within a religious tradition, they are among the Devout. If their ties to formal religions are relatively weak but they say they value self-fulfillment, personal growth, and human development, they are likely to be Altruists.

When exploring the life domain of *Friends* and associates, fund raisers should be alert to two dimensions. Each one specifies a different philanthropic personality. One is the importance of business contacts made possible through informal settings. The Communitarian will say that this issue is important. The other issue concerns social peers and charity functions. The philanthropic personality strongly focused on this issue is the Socialite.

The "life domain" methodology as applied to the various philanthropic personalities is summarized in the following list:

Family History

Tradition of giving	Dynasts
Situational change	Repayers

Financial Orientation

Monetary calculus	Investors

Fundamental Beliefs

Self-fulfillment	Altruists
Traditional religion	Devout

Friends and Associates

Business contacts   Communitarians
Social interactions   Socialites

This relatively simple and conversationally oriented approach allows fund raisers to come to a deeper understanding of an individual donor and to differentiate among the Seven Faces philanthropic personalities. Developing personal rapport with an affluent prospect is essential for this or any conversational approach to be effective. Rapport is best established by asking people to talk about themselves with an expression of sincere interest. Experienced fund raisers do this by asking a few questions to determine what the wealthy person is interested in. By incorporating a review of the life domains into the conversation, a fund raiser can, with comparative ease, determine a great deal of the wealthy person's psychology. Fund raisers can then use this information to more effectively position their organization. Once an affluent individual's Seven Faces philanthropic personality is ascertained, the next phase is to create a "Velcro" set of meaningful connections between these donor interests and the nonprofit mission and activities. This, the second phase in "Crafting the Vision," centers on language use, actual words and phrases, to create bridges of understanding.

Phase 2: Creating Bridges of Understanding

Fund raisers already know that different philanthropists give to nonprofits for different reasons, an insight confirmed by the Seven Faces research. The second phase to "Crafting the Vision" is to use specific positive images to communicate the mission and actions of a nonprofit to each type of prospective donor. When done well, this communication creates bridges of understanding. Decades of fund-raising experience, recently confirmed by empirical research (described in the Appendix), shows that different donor types respond favorably to different positive messages. These differences in message preferences represent focal points for nonprofits in communicating effectively with donors. The following section explores relationships between the positive images and the Seven Faces philanthropic personalities and provides examples culled from major donors that demonstrate their successful use in fund-raising situations.

How Positive Images Can Be Used to Build and Sustain Appeals to Different Philanthropic Personalities

Table 9.1 shows how the various faces responded to the positive image words presented to them. The table has been set up in a way to show its use. As an example, follow the Communitarian column down the length of the table. The positive images have been grouped according to their relevance and importance to Communitarians for this example. The first group includes the positive images important to the Communitarian type of major donor. A close reading of this list reveals three clusters of related words:

1. "Doing good," "social responsibility," and related concepts, which show an orientation toward philanthropy
2. "Accountability," "effectiveness," and the like, which show a preference for well-managed, businesslike nonprofits
3. "Local interests," "civic responsibility," and "supporting each other," which reveal a particular preference for locally oriented or community-minded nonprofits

Fund raisers can see that the Communitarian type is both similar to and distinct from other philanthropic personalities in terms of the positive images they respond to most. For example, the Communitarian and the Investor both rate the images of professionalism and quality of management high, although these images are slightly more important to Investors. However, Communitarians and Investors part company on the importance of an image of a nonprofit serving community needs. Images of a local orientation are extremely important to Communitarians, but are significantly less important to Investors.

Table 9.1. Responses to Positive Images
by Philanthropic Personality.

Positive images	Philanthropic personality						
	Communitarian	Devout	Investor	Socialite	Altruist	Repayer	Dynast
Responsibility	4	3	2	3	1	3	4
Service	4	4	2	2	1	4	1
Fund raising	4	2	3	4	1	2	1
Accountability	4	1	4	1	1	1	2
Effectiveness	4	1	4	1	1	4	3
Supporting each other	4	4	1	4	2	4	4
Local interests	4	1	1	1	1	1	1
Socially responsible	4	1	3	3	4	4	4
Good for community	4	2	2	3	1	2	2
Serving community	4	1	3	4	1	1	3
Leadership	4	1	4	4	1	1	2
Doing good	4	4	4	4	4	4	4
Opportunity	4	1	4	1	1	4	1
Civic responsibility	4	1	2	2	1	1	2
Results	3	1	4	1	1	2	2
Duty	3	4	1	3	1	2	2
Performance	3	1	4	2	1	2	2
Local economy	3	1	1	1	1	1	1
Efficiency	3	1	4	1	1	1	1
Well managed	3	1	4	1	1	1	1
Fellowship	3	3	1	4	1	1	2
God	2	4	2	2	1	2	2
Self-fulfillment	2	2	2	1	4	1	3
Fiduciary	2	1	4	1	1	1	2
Professional	2	1	4	1	1	1	1
Charity functions	2	2	1	4	1	1	2
Civic duty	2	1	1	2	1	1	1
Family tradition	1	2	1	2	1	1	4
Special event	1	1	1	4	1	3	1
Pay back	1	4	1	1	1	4	3
Good works	1	4	1	1	2	2	1
Sense of purpose	1	4	1	1	4	2	3
Obligation	1	3	1	1	1	2	3
Self-actualization	1	2	1	1	4	1	2
Gratitude	1	1	1	1	1	3	1
Grateful	1	1	1	1	1	4	2
Mission	1	4	1	1	4	3	1

Table 9.1. Responses to Positive Images
by Philanthropic Personality, Cont'd.

Positive images	Philanthropic personality						
	Communitarian	Devout	Investor	Socialite	Altruist	Repayer	Dynast
Faith	1	3	1	1	1	1	1
Difference in life	1	3	1	1	3	4	1
Family history	1	2	1	2	1	1	4
Vision	1	4	1	1	4	1	1
Value	1	4	1	1	1	1	1

Note: 4 = Extremely important; 3 = Important; 2 = Somewhat important; 1 = Not important.

Scanning the chart by running one's fingers down any two pairs of columns can reveal interesting points of convergence and divergence among the philanthropic personalities. For example, Altruists and the Devout are quite similar on many points—both groups rate such positive images as "service," "sense of purpose," "mission," and "vision" extremely high and images such as "civic responsibility," "local interests," "efficiency," and "performance" relatively low. However, the groups clearly divide in terms of the personal relevance of these positive images: "self fulfillment," "self-actualization," and "socially responsible." All are rated much higher by Altruists, and "God," "duty," "service," and "value" are rated much higher by the Devout.

Fund raisers who are donor-oriented in this way and who respond proactively to donors' needs and benefits by providing positive images of the nonprofit are good examples of the best in development through relationships. Relationship development starts from the premise that any effective long-term relationship—such as that between donor, fund raiser, and nonprofit—must be built on a foundation of mutual trust, understanding, and benefit. Fund raisers representing any successful nonprofit have many, many aspects to choose from in promoting the organization. The most successful fund raisers choose among these aspects for the set of positive images most relevant to the individual donor. A development officer for a world-class university, for example, could communicate hundreds of different activities, goals, successes, and the like. The point is that fund raisers make careful choices about what to emphasize, and to whom. The Seven Faces philanthropic personality strategy can help the university select positive images of what it does well and communicate those to the subgroup of prospective donors most likely to value it. Repayers will want to hear about positive images of achievements and programs within, say, the law or medical school or the science departments. Communitarians will welcome positive images of how they could help link promising students from their communities to scholarship programs. Socialites will respond favorably to participation in alumni fund raisers. Dynasts warm to positive images of endowing a new wing that will honor the three generations of family which have attended. The following sections provide examples philanthropists themselves offered, of actual cases where fund raisers successfully used positive imagery to connect them to a nonprofit. In the quotations which follow, donor use of positive images is highlighted. In addition, Table 9.2 extracts only the primary positive images for each philanthropic personality for ease of reference.

Repayers Respond to Positive Images That Evoke Their Specific Motivations

Of all the philanthropic personalities, Repayers have one of the most narrow sets of motivations for giving and are indifferent to, if not put off by, other reasons for supporting nonprofits. With Repayers, fund raisers know to take great care in identification, and then in communicating, reinforcing, understanding, and showing appreciation of their unique set of motivations.

Successful communications between fund raisers and

Table 9.2. Positive Images by Philanthropic Personality.

Philanthropic personality	Positive images	
Repayers	Pay back	Supporting each other
	Grateful	Made a difference in my life
	Effectiveness	Doing good
	Socially responsible	Opportunity
Communitarians	Responsibility	Supporting each other
	Service	Serving the community
	Fund raising	Civic responsibility
	Accountability	Leadership
	Socially responsible	Doing good
	Good for the community	Effectiveness
Socialites	Special event	Serving the community
	Charity functions	Leadership
	Fund raising	Doing good
	Supporting each other	Fellowship
Altruists	Self-fulfillment	Socially responsible
	Sense of purpose	Doing good
	Self-actualization	
Devout	God	Mission
	Duty	Doing good
	Service	Opportunity
	Sense of purpose	Good works
	Supporting each other	
Investors	Results	Efficiency
	Performance	Effectiveness
	Fiduciary	Well-managed
	Professional	Leadership
	Accountability	Opportunity
	Doing good	
Dynasts	Family tradition	Supporting each other
	Responsibility	Family history
	Socially responsible	Doing good

Repayer donors inevitably use wording which expresses their empathy with the Repayers' own experience: such phrases as "I can see that it made a difference in your life" are effective, as are those which link the Repayers' past experience to the experiences of others like them, such as "it's important to support each other," "finding opportunities to pay back," and "show you are grateful." These specific positive images are often supported with reinforcement for philanthropy in general. This reinforcement can be communicated using images such as "being socially responsible" and "doing good."

> I was real happy when Dick (from the university) took a lot of time talking with me about my years at school, and what I thought really *made the most difference* in my life later on. He then went and found out about a couple of new programs (in the school) that hooked up well with what mattered to me, and so he got my whole-hearted support. He never pushed stuff I wasn't interested in.

> I liked finding out that Samantha (the fundraiser) was also an alumna. She and I got to talking about a lot of different things about the school and how *much it meant to each of us.* Samantha helped me come to understand how, by giving, I could *make a difference* for someone else.

Communitarians Especially Respond to Three Positive Images — Community, Leadership, and Accountability

Communitarians need communications that include three positive images. First, they need to be reassured about the connections between the nonprofit and the local community. Communitarians need to hear from fund raisers that the nonprofit also shares such values as "civic responsibility," "serving the community," and "good for the community," and they need to hear this through positive images. Second, fund raisers should go out of their way to acknowledge the leadership role of the Communitarians in the community, and convey that the nonprofit, too, strives to embody such characteristics as "leadership," "responsibility," and "service." Finally, Communitarians need to feel that the nonprofit is well managed; fund raisers communicate assurances through positive images that managers of the nonprofit hold themselves "accountable." There are opportunities to reinforce each of these positive images in every conversation with a Communitarian, both by fund raisers and by other Communitarians in the prospect donor's charity network.

> I'm not out to save the whole world, just a small little slice, this *community* right here. I find that's what I think about, and that I gravitate to other people centered on the same things I am — *this city* and its county. John and Ann (fund raisers) each helped me connect the work they do to my interests, so that's why I am supporting this youth program and the shelter.

> This charity got my support when they got the support of some of the other high-placed *community leaders*. Frankly, I don't get involved in anything until *top people in the community* like Robert (president of the local Rotary Club) and Stan (prominent lawyer involved in county politics) and Carol (chairperson of the local Junior League) are behind it.

Positive Images to Socialites Reflect Mutual Support Through Fund Raising and Community Leadership

Fund raisers confirm that Socialites are fairly easy to identify and to frame positive messages for. Socialites see themselves as leaders of local groups who are skilled at mobilizing people and resources for a good cause, and Socialites are well aware that related social events cement relationships and reward volunteers and donors alike. Fund raisers should communicate positive images of "fund raising activities," "special events," and "charity functions" when describing activities of their nonprofit to Socialites, especially when these images are reinforced with messages of cooperative effort. Fund raisers also benefit by realizing that when Socialites choose to support a nonprofit, the decision is reinforced by their personal charity network — the same network Socialites rely on to fill committee assignments and to buy tables. By communicating positive images of "supporting each other," "serving the community," and "fellowship" to Socialites, fund raisers enhance their chances of success.

It was Herman (director of the charity) who got me talking about how I thought it was important to *serve the community* and *help others* through *fund raisers*.

While I am careful about what I take on, I do like it when fund raisers and directors talk to me about what it is that I do well. I am great at *fund raisers*. I want to *make the world a little better* and *help others*, and how I do that is through fund raisers for the charities I support. When I am approached about fund raisers, I am more apt to listen than if they want my involvement some other way.

Self-Fulfillment Is the Positive Image That Resonates Most with Altruists

Fund raisers benefit by knowing that Altruists are people who want to have an effect and seek out people and nonprofits who want to make a difference just as they do. Altruists respond favorably when positive images such as "self-fulfillment," "self-actualization," and "sense of purpose" are the dominant themes. Altruists sense kindred spirits in a nonprofit when words such as "vision" and "mission" are used in conversation to describe the goals and objectives of the organization. They also welcome messages which reinforce their general philanthropic predispositions, messages around the themes of "socially responsible" and "doing good."

I look for nonprofits with a *sense of vision,* who are intent on making a *better world,* where there is an almost palpable sense of *purpose* and energy.

I listen especially hard when fund raisers talk. I listen for them to give me a *vision* of where they are going and how *socially committed* people can fit in. If they can show me that, I'm reassured that I'm at the right place.

The Devout Prefer Positive Images Reinforcing Their Religious Rationale for Philanthropy

If the ideals and beliefs of fund raisers associated with the non-profit reflect their own deeply held religious beliefs, the Devout have an increased sense of confidence that the nonprofit is worth supporting. Fund raisers communicate more effectively with the Devout by using positive images drawn from the appropriate religious traditions and images that reflect their religious basis for philanthropy. These positive images include "God," "duty," "service," "mission," "values," and "vision."

> I know the nonprofit is worthy of my money and my time when they have fund raisers. I talk to enough to know that they have *God in their hearts.*

> The fund raisers and the other people who are with charity need to be doing it because they feel *Godly*, deep down *Godly.* When I found out that the people there have a weekly *Bible* breakfast with donors and volunteers, that's when I decided to come in.

Investors Look for Positive Images That Assure Them That the Nonprofit Is Efficient and Effective

Investors have broad interests with respect to the types of nonprofits they support, although they are inclined toward the same community-oriented organizations preferred by Communitarians and Socialites. Unlike those other two personalities, however, Investors focus on operations — business fundamentals. Fund raisers know that Investors want to hear positive images such as the sound financial management, the productivity, and the efficiency of the organization. Investors look for signals of professionalism and a businesslike approach in conversations with nonprofits.

> I always want to know about how they handle *accounting* and whether they are on top of their *books*. I need fund raisers to

> tell me whether the *money's* going where it's supposed to, to
> the programs and to the people who need it, and not to *ad-
> ministrative overhead.* I liked Judy (the fund raiser) coming
> right out with statistics showing me how they were *careful
> managers.*

> I listen hard to what the fund raisers' managers have to say, and
> I read all their material to see if they're interested in *results* and
> *accountability.*

Dynasts Need Positive Images Linking the Nonprofit to Their Upbringing in the World of Philanthropy

More than other philanthropic personalities, Dynasts move
in a charity network that is also a social class. Fund raisers
who are aware that older-generation Dynasts are significantly
influenced by the actions of others in their class, while newer-
generation Dynasts prefer making an independent mark in
the world of philanthropy, can improve their success rate.
Dynasts of any age tend to rely on their charity network and
respond positively to fund raisers who communicate their
appreciation of the unique status of Dynasts. Fund raisers
should communicate positive images that convey understanding of the "family tradition," "family history," and "responsibility" that motivate Dynasts. These communications are especially effective when reinforced with acknowledgement of
philanthropic motivations in general, such as "socially responsible," "supporting each other," and "doing good."

> When it comes to giving money away, I can identify with some-
> one who can identify with me. I prefer to work with fund raisers
> who understand the *special responsibility of family money.*

> Alan is a model fundraiser. He knows just how to respect that
> our *tradition of giving* goes back *generations,* and that I know what
> I'm doing.

Phase 3: Testimonials and Endorsements

Social influence theory explains that one of the means by which people identify a correct course of action is to refer to the behavior of others (Cialdini, 1984). When people look to others, the feedback they obtain can be called a testimonial. Obtaining testimonials is a way people making important decisions gain confidence in their course of action. Prospective donors are people making important decisions, and testimonials help donors feel more confident and assured about their decisions.

Most often, testimonials take the form of word-of-mouth, in which a person considering a decision will seek out others to obtain their opinions. An Investor, for example, who seeks to create a charitable remainder trust will perceive this as a complex and risky task (there are, of course, severe tax consequences if the trust is not properly executed). Under these conditions, Investors will naturally want to check with people like themselves—other Investors—on the specific construction of the planned gift mechanism. A Communitarian who becomes involved with a charity his peer group will not support can be exposed to significant business as well as social consequences; to avoid such negative consequences, Communitarians rarely make a major nonprofit-related decision without checking with others like themselves. Not all donors rely on testimonials. For example, since Altruists are driven by internal needs and criteria, they are comparatively unattached to outcomes and therefore rely less on testimonials than other philanthropic personalities.

The effectiveness of testimonials is enhanced when they originate from people of higher status, with whom there is emotional identification or a high degree of perceived similarity. If the person providing the testimonial not only shares some basic similarities but also is seen as carrying greater status, then the likelihood of influencing behavior is heightened. All wealthy philanthropists, to varying degrees, are influenced by the people in their charity network with whom they identify (Figure 9.1).

Figure 9.1. The Power of Testimonials.

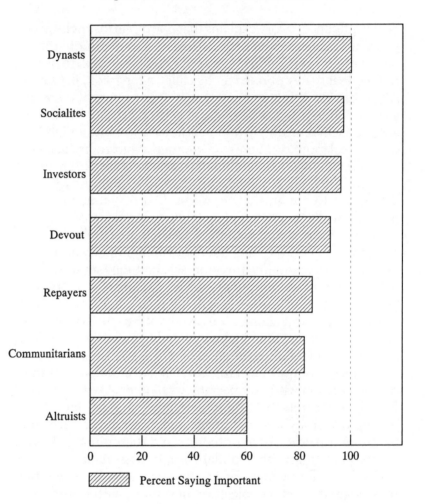

Percent Saying Important

While Dynasts are the most influenced and Altruists the least, this process of identification with other donors is powerful. For the wealthy philanthropist, reaching out to other donors to solicit testimonials occurs because it is an efficient and unobtrusive method of evaluating the nonprofit. The logic, somewhat simplified, goes: If so-and-so is involved, I must be making a good decision to also become involved because so-and-so would only become involved with a charitable organization of the highest quality.

> When I saw all those famous people at the gala, I knew this charity was a class act. Frankly, it helped me decide to support them, too.
> —*A Socialite*

> I have a lot of respect for some of the people in this city. When I found out Ann and Dick were part of the children's education group, well, that convinced me that it was a quality organization.
> —*A Communitarian*

> I had this general feeling I owed the school something, but I didn't do anything about it until I saw people I knew were already members of the President's club. That did it. I figured if Bob thought it was a good place to put his money, I felt confident that it was a good place to put mine.
> —*A Repayer*

Testimonials to prospective donors from long-term donors are the key to establishing relationships between nonprofits and wealthy philanthropists. The person best suited to provide an appropriate testimonial for one philanthropic personality is someone of the same philanthropic personality who is already involved with the nonprofit. That is, Repayers are most influenced by other Repayers, Communitarians by Communitarians, and so forth. Prospective donors also become attached to nonprofits through identification with others like themselves who are major supporters of the charity. Providing the linkage between the two groups and facilitating communication of testimonials is one of the fund raiser's most effective roles.

> I knew what I wanted to do, I just wasn't so sure which charity would do the best job. When Sue-Ann (the development officer) had me meet Douglas and Mike, that really helped me make up my mind. They are people like me, and they were involved with

this one charity, so I asked them about it. What they said made
a lot of sense, so I asked Sue-Ann to help me get involved.
                              — A *Communitarian*

I make up my own mind. Still, it is very reassuring to check out
a charity with a few people and get the good word back. It gives
me a good feeling all over that I'm doing the right thing.
                              An Investor

Implications

The process of creating a relationship with a prospective
major donor is a demanding one. Once donor awareness of
the nonprofit is created through leveraging the charity networks, fund raisers should turn to the next stage, the stage
of building donor commitment through "Crafting the Vision."
"Crafting the Vision" is an interpersonal process with three
key steps: (1) use life domains to identify the donor by their
characteristic Seven Faces philanthropic personality, (2) create bridges of understanding with the donor with positive
images, and (3) build commitment through the testimonials
of other donors of the same philanthropic personality.

Use Life Domains to Identify
Philanthropic Personalities

- Solicit major gifts and the varieties of support from the
  affluent through a one-to-one process. This requires a
  conversation-based means of identifying each philanthropic personality.
- Work through the life domains in conversation with an
  affluent prospect.
    The *Family* history life domain identifies the Dynast who
        has a tradition of giving as well as the Repayer for
        whom there has been a significant situational change.
    The life domain of *Financial* orientation can expose
        the use of a monetary calculus in philanthropic de-
        cisions, thus identifying the Investor.

> The life domain of *Fundamental* beliefs uncovers both the Altruist and the Devout; if the emphasis is religious, the donor is a Devout. If the emphasis is on the importance of personal self-fulfillment, the prospective donor is an Altruist.
>
> In the *Friends* and associates life domain, the relative importance of informal business contacts reveals the Communitarian, while an expressed importance of social peers and charity functions unveils the Socialite.

- Recognizing that the life domain framework is a convenient summary of the philanthropic personalities, but a comprehensive understanding of all seven faces as detailed in Part One is essential.

Build Bridges of Understanding by Using Positive Images

- Choose positive images to position the nonprofit as meeting the philanthropic needs of the major donors.
- Reinforce positive images in important communications with the donor.

Validate the Perceptions of Philanthropists Through Testimonials

- Testimonials are the optimal source of social validation for a prospective philanthropist.
- The best testimonial for a donor is another individual with the same philanthropic personality.

10

Identifying Appropriate Giving Strategies

I wish I had a better grasp of *how* I could give. If I did, I feel
I could do much more for the nonprofit. I feel like all I know
how to do is write a check and I know there are other ways of
giving money like trusts and such.
—*A Repayer*

I hear there are lots of different ways to give. I would be real
interested in finding out more about foundations and trusts. I
feel a little sad I've had such a short-term view of it all. I'd like
to see other possibilities.
—*A Communitarian*

As experienced fund raisers know, the key to promoting
charitable giving strategies is to go slow and build up to
major gifts over time. This is common sense and also good
psychology. Psychologists have found that people generally
like to get accustomed to relationships and new arrangements
on a gradual and incremental basis. This psychological insight has been applied to buyer behavior through a construct
known as foot-in-the-door theory. Foot-in-the-door theory,
which has proven useful in many situations where people
feel their competence and knowledge is low while risk is high,

states that people find it easier to make small commitments at first in order to manage risk and uncertainty. As we have seen, donors express some concern about the uncertainties and risks associated with the making of major gifts.

Applied to development situations, foot-in-the-door theory calls for a process of carefully sequenced strategies for increasing the involvement of a prospective donor over time. As fund raisers know, it is the rare philanthropist who makes a major gift without a prior relationship with a nonprofit. The typical success story a development officer will share involves a donor who began with a modest cash donation, attended a benefit fund raiser or two, was invited to tour facilities, joined a committee, participated in an annual giving campaign, increased personal donations, and ultimately created a trust benefiting the nonprofit. Implicit in foot-in-the-door theory is the need to continually educate the customer about the product being sold in order to reduce perceived risk, heighten feelings of personal competence and knowledge, and also create involvement. The implication for development, of course, is to educate the donor about the activities and programs of the nonprofit. It also means, however, educating the donor about the various charitable giving strategies available to them. Because public policy is to promote philanthropy, a wide range of financial and legal instruments are available to donors and their advisors. These instruments range from the simple to the complex, from giving of tangible and intangible property, planned giving strategies consisting of life insurance, charitable bequests, gift annuities, pooled income funds, charitable remainder trusts, charitable lead trusts, donor-advised funds at community foundations, to the creation of private foundations.

Of course, not every donor is equally interested in each type of giving strategy. It can be a challenge to identify the donor's interests to begin the awareness building and educational process. The Seven Faces framework provides insight into the types of giving strategies which interest different groups of donors. This is, of course, the objective of segmentation strategies. Successful strategies should break a large group—such as all donors—into smaller groups, or segments, which are similar in the way they approach an encounter with a service provider. Thus, we would expect to find that Communitarians differ from Dynasts in the kinds of charitable giving strategies they are familiar with, and that both differ from Repayers. As the following sections will show, the seven philanthropic personalities are, in fact, very different from one another along three dimensions: they differ in familiarity with the various charitable giving strategies; they differ in their views of the extent nonprofits have promoted various strategies to them; and they differ in their interest in learning more about various options open to them. The Seven Faces framework reveals that significant opportunities exist for fund raisers willing to effectively position the more technically complex giving strategies.

This pattern of differences by Seven Faces segment is described in the text and illustrated in charts. Figure 10.1 shows that many major donors are not familiar with giving strategies other than cash. Figure 10.2 shows that only the most sophisticated nonprofits appear to emphasize planned giving strategies to their potential donors; bequests are the only gifting strategy other than current giving associated with some awareness, and even that familiarity is specific to only some segments. Figure 10.3 shows that significant new opportunity is available to fund raisers, as donor interest in becoming more familiar with many available options is widespread. Two options in particular—private foundations and planned giving using charitable remainder trusts—interest current donors.

Implicit in this process are the fundamental skills of effective fund raising, especially those of guiding the donor to the point of commitment. The not-inconsiderable skill of "making the ask" is well covered in any number of other books on fund raising and so is not discussed here. Indeed, successful application of the Seven Faces approach assumes that these basic fund-raising competencies are in place.

Figure 10.1. Donor Familiarity
with Charitable Giving Strategies.

Percent Responding "Some" or "Very Interested"

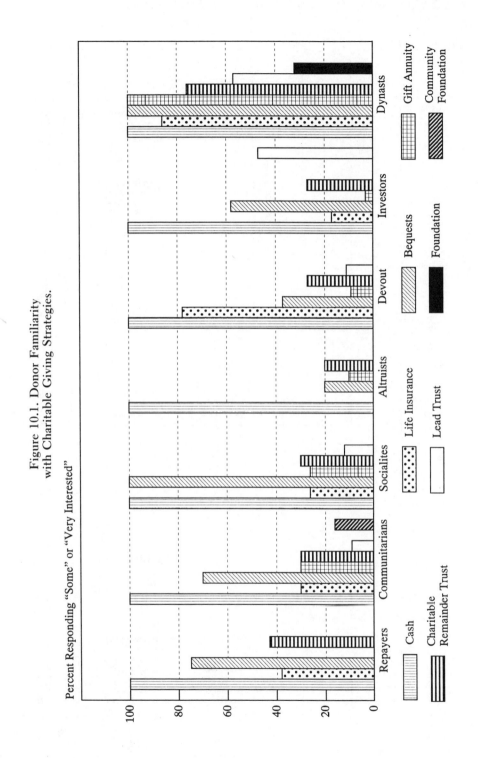

Cash

Charitable
Remainder Trust

Life Insurance

Lead Trust

Bequests

Foundation

Gift Annuity

Community
Foundation

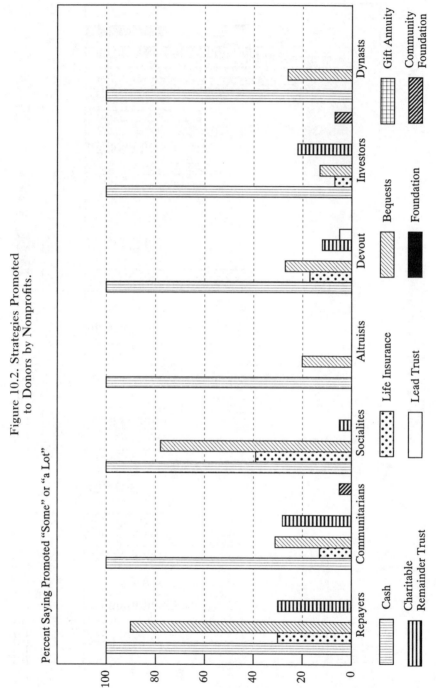

Figure 10.2. Strategies Promoted to Donors by Nonprofits.

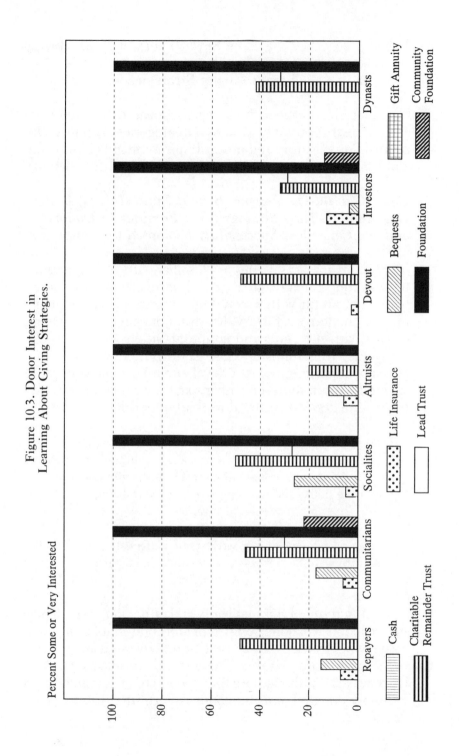

Figure 10.3. Donor Interest in
Learning About Giving Strategies.

Current Giving Strategies

Current giving, particularly cash gifts, appears to be extensively and successfully promoted across all categories of donors. Opportunities exist for fund raisers to promote gifts of tangible and intangible property, planned gifts, and private foundations.

Cash (Capital Campaigns, Benefit Fund Raisers) Is the Charitable Gifting Strategy Most Familiar to Donors and the One Most Successfully Promoted by Nonprofits

All philanthropists say they are familiar with cash donations to nonprofits; all also say that cash gifts are well promoted by the nonprofits with which they interact. This form of giving has the longest history. Most donors begin their giving careers with such gifts and nonprofits find such giving relatively easy to administer. Cash contributions are also strategically important in donor development programs because such gifts often represent the initial donor relationship, the foot-in-the-door to future donor interactions.

> I was initially approached for a cash contribution, so that's what I did. It seemed logical at the time, and I didn't mind. It gave me an opportunity to find out more about the group and what they were doing and how effective they were being.
> — *An Investor*

> I began my giving with just writing out a check. It's simple and straightforward, and it was easy for me to get started.
> — *A Socialite*

As a result of this familiarity and rather long experience, major donors feel quite competent and comfortable with their cash-giving strategies. As a result, none expressed any interest in learning more about it. The general consensus was that there wasn't anything more that needed to be learned — cash is simply donated and the donor is permitted to take a tax deduction.

It's all straightforward. What's there to know about making a charitable contribution?
— An Altruist

Levels of Current Awareness of Tangible Property Are Mixed Among the Philanthropic Styles; There Is Limited Donor Interest in Learning More, So Such Gifts Are Infrequently Promoted by Nonprofits

Familiarity with ways of making tangible gifts (such as real estate, art, and antiques) to charities is quite mixed among major donors. Repayers and Altruists say they have no real familiarity with such gifts, while only 7.0 percent of Communitarians and 17.4 percent of Socialites say they are familiar to some extent with such gifts. Investors, the Devout, and Dynasts are generally more familiar (59.4%, 64.4%, and 93.8%, respectively). As will be seen repeatedly in this chapter, Dynasts have the greatest overall familiarity with the many types of charitable giving strategies due to their family tradition and their greater personal experience in giving.

Gifts of tangible property is not an area that appeals to most potential major donors. In fact, none of these philanthropists expressed any interest in learning more about making such gifts. Fund raisers have also picked up on this lack of interest. Donors agree that few fund raisers have approached them about the benefits of tangible gifts.

I want to help the nonprofits I have chosen, and to me that means helping them pay the bills. Unless there's something special that I'm missing about a gift of real estate or some other thing, I really don't want to know about that option.
— A Repayer

Frankly, property isn't something I have ever thought about giving. To come to think about it, I can't remember that anyone at church has ever talked about it. It just doesn't seem done.
— A Devout

Gifts of Intangible Property Are Appealing to Only
Two Donor Types—Communitarians and Investors

Because they are interested in gifts of intangible property
(such as stock), Investors and Communitarians stand out from
the other philanthropic personalities. About half the Investors (46.9%) are familiar with intangible property as gifts, and
a quarter (25.0%) would like to learn more. Fund raisers are
beginning to act on this opportunity; 23.2 percent of Investors say gifts of intangible property have been actively promoted to them by the nonprofits with which they deal. Communitarians are not quite as familiar with the category as
Investors although interest in learning more about such opportunities runs almost as high among Communitarians
(22.8%) as among Investors. Fewer, however, recall being approached by nonprofits for gifts of intangible property (5.3%).

The appeal of a giving strategy of intangible property
is that Investors and Communitarians are often business
owners. In making gifts of intangible property, they see opportunity to utilize their greatest asset—their businesses—
in a charitable fashion.

> I have a private company and the idea of using stock in the com-
> pany as a charitable gift has piqued my interest.
> —*A Communitarian*

> I want to learn more about how to give stock in my company
> to charity. I think it's a great idea, and I'd like to find someone
> who can do a good job of explaining it.
> —*An Investor*

Most Dynasts (85.0%) are familiar with gifts of intangible property and thus express almost no interest in learning
more about this strategy. Sensing this, nonprofits do not promote such gifts intensively to Dynasts. All the other philanthropic personalities are neither very familiar with nor particularly interested in learning more about gifts of intangible
property.

Planned Giving Strategies

Planned giving, by its nature, tends to come later in the relationship process between donor and nonprofit, tends to involve larger gifts, and tends to be more complex because of the intricacies of the giving strategies coupled with the donor's personal financial considerations. The making of a planned gift usually involves the participation of the donors' personal legal and/or financial advisor. In addition, the available range of products is wider.

In general, donor familiarity with planned giving strategies is spotty. There is, however, a high degree of interest among philanthropists in learning more about planned giving, in particular in learning about charitable remainder trusts. The need for more information and education in planned giving which donors express is already being seized upon by trend-setting fund raisers.

In Spite of the Fact That Bequests Are the Most Heavily Promoted of All Planned Giving Products, Familiarity with Bequests Ranges Widely

Familiarity with bequests varies greatly. Those least aware include Altruists (20.0%) and the Devout (35.5%). Substantial proportions of Investors (59.4%), Communitarians (70.2%), and Repayers (76.2%) say they are familiar with bequests, as are all (100.0%) Socialites and Dynasts. Fund raisers are particularly effective when promoting bequests to some segments; a high proportion of Repayers (91.5%) and Socialites (78.2%) have had substantial interactions with development officers on bequest issues.

> Sam (the medical center foundation head) is doing a good job, I think. It gets mentioned to me regularly that I could really benefit the hospital if I left them something in my will.
> —A Repayer

> My friends and I have talked about leaving something to our favorite charities in our wills. And, the nonprofit people bring

it up once in a while in a nice way. I'm going to be sitting down
with my lawyer about it.

                                        — A *Socialite*

There is some interest in learning more about bequests
on the part of some segments, principally Socialites (26.0%),
Communitarians (15.8%), Repayers (14.3%), and Altruists
(10.0%). Donors want to be familiar with the advantages and
disadvantages of bequests as compared to the other planned
giving strategies. This need for information is beginning to
be met by nonprofits as more donors say fund raisers have
promoted bequests to them as a giving option. Nonprofit-
provided materials and input have been used by about a third
(31.6%) of Communitarians, about a quarter of the Devout
(26.7%) and Dynasts (25.0%), and to a lesser degree by Altruists (20.0%) and Investors (12.5%).

Awareness of Life Insurance as a Charitable Giving Strategy Varies; Although Some Nonprofits Promote the Option, Interest in Learning More Is Low

Awareness of life insurance as a charitable giving option ranges
from nonexistent among Altruists (0%) to near universal
among Dynasts (87.6%), with other philanthropic personalities
in between — Investors (15.6%), Socialites (26.1%), Communitarians (29.8%), Repayers (38.1%), and the Devout (77.7%).

Interest in learning more about life insurance as a charitable giving strategy is low; in no segment did more than 12.5
percent express a medium or high degree of interest. The usual
customer resistance to buying life insurance is also present
even if a nonprofit is the beneficiary. Donors, like people
generally, are uncomfortable with the life insurance product.
Only a few philanthropists report that a life insurance option
was raised with them by a nonprofit, and they were generally
put off by the notion. Since major donors are wealthy people
with extensive investment and financial management experience, they also tend to believe that other instruments have
advantages over life insurance as an investment.

> Frankly, I don't like insurance because I have always viewed it as a poor investment. If I were going to do a planned gift, it would not be with insurance.
>
> —A *Communitarian*

> This may be foolish, but I have always felt uncomfortable with life insurance policy. It just makes me feel as though everyone would be sitting around waiting for me to die. I know that's not true, but it makes me feel uneasy.
>
> —A *Socialite*

Fund raisers have picked up on this ambivalence toward life insurance as a planned giving vehicle. As a result, the degree to which life insurance is promoted to donors by fund raisers is generally low and variable. In only the Socialite donor group does more than a third recall a nonprofit promoting life insurance (39.1%). Most other groups believe that promotion of life insurance has been infrequent—Repayers (28.6%), the Devout (15.6%), Communitarians (10.5%), Investors (6.3%), and no Dynasts or Altruists.

There Is Little Interest in Gift Annuities Among Major Donors

As usual, Dynasts were the group most familiar with gift annuities (100%). Awareness of this planned giving option is much lower across the other groups—Communitarians (29.8%), Socialites (26.1%), Altruists (10.0%), the Devout (8.9%), and Investors (3.1%).

Wealthy givers have little interest in gift annuities; as a result, fund raisers infrequently promote gift annuities. In part, this may be because gift annuities tend to be perceived as a mass market form of planned giving, a form in which individual attention to the donor's financial needs is not forthcoming due to the nature of the product (Prince, 1991).

> If I'm going to do planned giving, it has to meet my financial needs and they're unique. I don't want a cookie cutter type

approach, which is what I think of when I think gift annuity.
For me, the planned giving approach has to be able to take this
all into account.
> —An Investor

I know all about gift annuities, and I won't use them because
they don't fit my position—my personal position, my financial
position. It doesn't seem to fit the way I like to give.
> —A Dynast

None of the donors in this study express any particular interest in learning more about gift annuities. Fund raisers
are aware that major donors lack interest in gift annuities
and do not promote them to any major degree.

Three Segments Are Well Aware of Pooled Income Funds, but Interest Is Low

Three philanthropic personalities are quite aware of pooled income funds—Dynasts (62.5%), Communitarians (52.7%), and
Investors (43.8%). In all other segments, reported awareness
is nonexistent. There is an across-the-board lack of interest
in pooled income funds among donors; as a result, fund raisers
do little promotion of pooled income funds as a planned giving
alternative. Only a small proportion of the Devout (2.2%) recall
ever discussing the option with a development professional.

Like gift annuities, donors seem to perceive pooled income funds as not fitting their individual needs. Although
such funds fulfill an important fund raising role for some nonprofits, some donors do not feel pooled income funds are
oriented to their needs.

If I'm going to do a planned gift, I certainly wouldn't use a pooled
income fund. Not with the money we're talking about.
> —A Dynast

Considering the other options I have looked into for this gift,
a pooled income fund just doesn't make a whole lot of sense to
me, and that's the advice the charity gave me, too.
> —An Investor

The limited appeal of a pooled income fund is well recognized among fund raisers; they do not devote time or energy in promoting the approach.

> I once brought up the idea of contributing to the Center's pooled income fund. Barney (Director) explained that in my case there were better ways of giving, and took the time to walk me through the different options. He was right, and I appreciated it.
> — A Devout

> In the charity I am on the board of, we set up a pooled income fund for those people who wanted certain advantages planned giving provides but couldn't give a lot. Our development director never promotes the fund to our wealthier benefactors.
> — A Communitarian

There Is Limited Awareness or Interest in Charitable Lead Trusts

A charitable lead trust provides an income stream for a nonprofit for a number of years. The assets of the trust then revert back to the donor or to some other noncharitable beneficiary.

Although a fair proportion of Dynasts are familiar with charitable lead trusts (56.3%), most other donors are not. Just a few Socialites (13.0%), Devout (11.1%), and Communitarians (8.8%) say they understand charitable lead trusts; the other segments do not. However, interest in learning about charitable lead trusts is relatively high, as it is with trusts generally. Interest in charitable lead trusts is the result of the sizable interest in charitable remainder trusts, for which familiarity is greater (refer to the section on charitable remainder trusts). In four segments, more than 20 percent said they would be interested in learning more (31.1% of Dynasts, 30.9% of Communitarians, 28.2% of Investors, 26.1% of Socialites). Very few Devout (2.2%) made the same statement. Fund raisers are beginning to respond to this upsurge of interest in trust strategies; the opportunity for promotion of trust options is high given the interest. A major opportunity exists in that relatively few fund raisers actively promote charitable lead trusts to their major donors who are planned giving prospects. Only a few of the Devout (4.4%) say they are aware of any development program involving this strategy.

> I would be interested in learning something about all the different kinds of charitable trusts. From what I know they seem like an excellent way of giving to charity.
> — An Investor

> My family used both remainder and lead trusts and I have to admit I'm not too sure about how each one works. It's something I would certainly be interested in learning about.
> — A Dynast

A Donor-Advised Fund in a Community Foundation Was Appealing to Communitarians and, to a Lesser Degree, to Investors

In the case of donor-advised funds in a community foundation as a planned giving strategy, only Communitarians and Investors are familiar with it, and only these two philanthropic styles had had discussions with fund raisers about implementation issues and only these two are interested in learning more. The previous chapter described the communication bridges specific words and images could provide. For Communitarians, a primary word is "community"; Investors, to a lesser extent, respond positively to the same message. Thus, Communitarians and Investors both want to learn more about the possibilities of donor-advised funds within a community foundation (21.1% and 12.9%, respectively). The same two segments are the only ones which recall nonprofit promotion of the strategy (3.5% and 6.3%, respectively), and this recall is, in part, a function of the shared image and belief in community development.

> At the Rotary Club we have someone from the Community Foundation come in and speak from time to time, so I am aware

of what they do. The idea of this kind of gift has always appealed
to me.

—A Communitarian

All other philanthropic styles are unfamiliar with donor-
advised funds for community foundations and say they are
not interested in learning more.

Next to Foundations, Charitable Remainder
Trusts Generate the Most Donor Interest

Interest in charitable remainder trusts (CRTs) is relatively
high in all donor segments; only private foundations generate more interest. Donors are already about as aware of
charitable remainder trusts as they are of bequests. Familiarity
with charitable remainder trusts is highest among Dynasts
(75.0%), followed by Repayers (42.9%), Socialites (30.4%),
Communitarians (29.8%), Investors (28.1%), the Devout
(26.6%), and Altruists (20.0%).

There is considerable interest among donors to know
more. Between a fifth and a half of philanthropists express
a medium to high interest in learning more about charitable
remainder trusts. Altruists (20.0%), Investors (31.2%), Dynasts
(42.8%), the Devout (46.7%), Communitarians (46.7%), Repayers (47.6%), and Socialites (47.8%). This elevated level
of interest, particularly when compared to other strategies,
represents significant opportunity for fund raisers.

Fund raisers are responding to donor needs, but donor
interest is outpacing fund raisers' response. These findings
show that current promotional efforts involving charitable
remainder trusts by nonprofits lag behind donor interest. Solid
proportions of Investors (21.9%), Communitarians (28.1%),
and Repayers (28.6%) have discussed charitable remainder
trusts with fund raisers, and smaller proportions of Socialites
(4.3%), the Devout (11.1%) have. Dynasts and Altruists say
that fund raisers have never discussed charitable remainder
trusts with them.

As fund raisers gear up to intensely promote charitable

remainder trusts, they should understand they have natural allies in the legal and financial communities. Charitable remainder trusts provide considerable financial benefits to these advisors as well as to donors and to nonprofits (Prince, 1992).

> My insurance agent has shown me how I can leave a very large gift to the Church and can get some financial advantages as well. We are scheduling a time to get together to get this thing started.
> — A *Devout*

> "Robert, my lawyer, introduced me to the charitable remainder trust. It's such a good thing I can't understand why everyone isn't doing it, and I am recommending it to other people.
> — A *Socialite*

At the current time, financial and legal advisors are promoting the CRT giving strategy in direct mail campaigns, print advertising, and by educating their affluent clientele to the service.

> I keep seeing things about charitable (remainder) trusts in the mail I get from my broker and now I hear about other people doing them. It gets me curious and I now want to learn something about them.
> — An *Altruist*

> I don't know much about charitable remainder trusts, but everyone seems to be talking about them. I would certainly be interested in learning more.
> — A *Repayer*

Foundations Generate Universal Interest, Far Outpacing Familiarity and Development Efforts

Every donor included in the study expressed at least moderate interest in learning more about foundations as a charitable giving strategy. While it is unlikely that every major donor surveyed is going to establish a foundation, all are quite interested in learning more about foundations as an option.

This extremely high indication of donor interest is just now breaking. Relatively few philanthropists would rate themselves expert on the options private foundations offer them as charitable giving vehicles. Indeed, only Dynasts say they are at least somewhat familiar (31.3%), a level of familiarity and expertise far lower than Dynasts reported on the other options.

> I hear great things about having a personal foundation. I suspect some of it is hype and some of it is true. I would like to know what's wheat and what's chaff.
> — *An Investor*

> My family has always been philanthropically inclined. We have a fair amount of money, but we're not Rockefellers or Carnegies. I would love to have a family foundation but we don't have hundreds of millions to put into it. People tell me we don't need amounts like that. It would be great just knowing the facts.
> — *A Dynast*

Because interest is so high and knowledge is relatively low, a great opportunity exists for fund raisers to educate donors in the intricacies and benefits of creating a private foundation. Some development directors have been reluctant to promote foundations since there is no guarantee that foundation funds will be channeled to any particular nonprofit. However, the extremely high interest shown by major donors in foundations suggests that nonprofits should develop a donor development strategy which includes the opportunity for donors to become more knowledgeable about these options.

> The idea of a private foundation is very appealing. It would be a real plus to learn more about private foundations, and I would like to talk it over with someone familiar with all the gifting options. Not only am I interested but all my friends are too.
> — *A Socialite*

> I have heard that the nonprofits are worried that if I had a foundation they would end up getting only some of my money. Well,

that's the way it is now. What makes them think that having a
foundation will make it any different? I'd rather work through
my options with a top notch fundraiser among my advisors, and
if it came out that it should be a foundation, I'd think well of
the fundraiser, and show it.

—An Investor

The affluent also perceive a number of benefits in establishing a private foundation. They believe a foundation may be
an effective vehicle to bring members closer together in a higher
purpose. They also think foundations would be a vital way
to include other family members in philanthropic activities.

I taught my children about running the business and I'm start-
ing to feel confident that they will do a good job. I'm sorry I never
paid more attention to teaching them how to give away money.
I think being a good donor is just as hard as running a business.
I think the idea of a foundation would make for a great environment in which to teach them about giving.

—An Investor

The more I hear about them the more I believe that a foundation
can get the whole family involved in philanthropy. It can be a
place where everyone learns to become more through charity.

—An Altruist

Implications

Philanthropists are generally aware that there are alternatives
to current giving, but feel generally ill-equipped to explore
these further without the support of knowledgeable fund
raisers and expert legal and financial advisors.

Fund Raisers Should Educate Philanthropists on the Various Charitable Giving Strategies

- The key to promoting current and planned giving strategies to the affluent, and to other donors for that matter,
  is education.

- Major donors are interested in becoming more familiar with certain giving strategies, in particular charitable remainder trusts and private foundations.
- Fundraisers who educate donors on these products demonstrate sincere concern and interest.
  - Such a tangible focus on the best interests of donors translates into a stronger relationship between the philanthropist and the fund raiser and the nonprofit.
  - The educational process, when properly implemented, also exposes major donors to ways they can give that they previously did not consider.
  - It is also advantageous to inform wealthy donors of giving strategies even though they may not be particularly attractive to them personally. As members of the charity network, the affluent may very well be able to promote these services to others.
  - Informing donors of giving strategies is especially important when donors themselves are enlisted in the fund-raising effort. By being educated about giving strategies, a major donor is positioned to recommend a suitable way for someone else to give.
- The educational process is a form of "charitable gift awareness development." As fund raisers educate affluent donors to the ways they can make charitable gifts, donors will impart this information throughout their network.
  - In effect, the nonprofit is training its "sales force."
  - It is important to note that this education is desired by wealthy donors who want to know about the different giving strategies.
  - Moreover, the affluent, in general, will eagerly talk about their philanthropy and concurrently be capable of informing their audience as to the way they can help.

Establish a Program of Strategic Alliances with Advisors to the Affluent

- Nonprofits should respond to the trend toward increased use of advisors among the affluent.

- Nonprofits benefit through relationships to advisors by referring clients in need of specialized professional services.
- Nonprofits also benefit from the relationship because they can serve donors more completely without creating the required expertise internally.
- In addition, because advisors also participate in the charity network, they may be a source of new referrals of donors.

Marketing of Charitable Remainder Trusts Should Be Personality as Well as Benefit-Oriented

- Donors of charitable remainder trusts can benefit in eight ways:
    The ability to provide a nonprofit with a future charitable gift
    An income tax deduction
    The opportunity to reduce or eliminate estate taxes
    The possibility of avoiding capital gains taxes
    The option to create a current or future revenue stream
    The opportunity to have assets compound tax free
    The ability to protect assets from creditors
    The recourse to ensure an inheritance for heirs
- Linking the meaning of philanthropy (as experienced by each philanthropic personality) to these product-specific benefits will help nonprofits promote charitable remainder trusts effectively.
- Fund raisers can educate advisors in the specific marketing skills and philanthropic advantages of charitable remainder trusts.
    Promoting only the financial benefits of the charitable remainder trust, a common fault among financial advisors, is only reasonably effective for Investors.
    When financials are the crux of the presentation made to the Devout or Altruists among other personalities, negative response patterns against the advisor and the nonprofit often result.

Nonprofits Should Establish a Program to Assist
Major Donors in the Establishment of Foundations

- The extremely high interest shown by major donors in private foundations suggests that nonprofits would be well advised to develop donor development strategies which include the opportunity for wealthy donors to become more knowledgeable about this option.
- Fund raisers' fears of losing control over donor dollars need to be overcome.
    Fund-raising executives often view promoting a private foundation as counterproductive to that goal.
    However, because of their widespread interest in foundations, the affluent can be expected to act. When they do, nonprofits can either be part of the process or left out of it.
    The wealthy are unlikely to stop funding a nonprofit they care about because they have established a private foundation; they will channel the funds differently.
- The affluent associate a number of nonfinancial benefits with foundations, among them:
    It is a viable giving strategy.
    A family foundation can result in greater cohesion within the family, a product of cooperating to achieve a higher purpose.
    It can be the vehicle to bring other family members into the world of philanthropy.
    It can exist in perpetuity, and as such it becomes a symbol of the charity of the donor forever.
- The same strategy of educating affluent donors to the viability of the charitable remainder trust should be applied to private foundations.
    This process will also require the use of financial and legal advisors outside the nonprofit.
    Once again, by establishing strategic alliances with advisors, not only are needed areas of expertise provided, but a potential referral source of new major donors is established.

- An additional benefit of working closely with those philanthropists who establish private foundations is the opportunity to create relationships with their children.

    Because Dynasts tend to seek out different nonprofits
    than their parents did, fund raisers may establish ties
    with the younger generation by working with them
    through a foundation.

    A nonprofit has a better opportunity to retain these
    future major donors by assisting them in learning
    how to give.

11

Sustaining Relationships Through Donor Centered Strategies

Ernie has knit me deeply into the fabric of the charity. He calls
before board meetings so I know what is happening. Afterwards,
he calls to get my opinion. He asks me to suggest things. I like
feeling useful, and needed.
                    — *A Dynast*

Looking back, I can see that I gave to a lot of different charities.
The ones I gave again to, however, are the ones who went out
of their way to get me involved in the little as well as the big
things.
                    — *A Communitarian*

A theme emerging again and again in this work is that major
donors respond positively to nonprofits who recognize and
attend to their Philanthropic Personality by creating opportunities for individual involvement. Donors want help in being channeled into roles most appropriate for their strengths,
and they want an ongoing relationship built on mutual benefit. For their part, fund raisers also want ongoing relationships with major donors, as the process of recruiting new
donors of any significant size is arduous.

    The creating and sustaining positive nonprofit-donor

relationships is the core of successful fund raising among major donors. Relationship development focuses on the specific interactions that motivate a customer to remain in the relationship, to invest further in the relationship through additional support, and to encourage others to support the nonprofit as well. When done well, successful relationship development is brought about by seeking win-win, mutually beneficial relationships over time (Kotler, 1991). This new focus on relationships is receiving considerable attention in other areas where the affluent are an important market (Morgan and Chadha, 1993; Illingworth, 1991; Ferguson and Brown, 1991), including fund raising (Ensman, 1992). The interest in stronger relationships with supporters is due to increasing competition for resources while the resource pool is diminishing (Brown and Swartz, 1989).

The relationship development process often begins with the adoption of a donor orientation (Congram and Dumesic, 1986). In many nonprofits, heightened awareness of donor needs is achieved with an educational program. The objectives of such an educational program are to raise the awareness of all organization members and to train personnel in the specific skills of relationship development (Gronroos, 1990; George, 1990).

> I have found that there are still some charities that just try to sell me on what they do. They just go on and on about their programs and their activities. When they do that, it makes me feel as though they aren't really interested in me, or in finding out about the way I might like to fit in. I have found some wonderful charities that have helped me get involved in just the ways that are comfortable for me.
> —A *Socialite*

> Because of my history (cancer), I only care about doing things for other women, but the development director keeps talking to me about the new wing for children he is trying to get underwritten. I know it is a good cause, but it's not *my* cause.
> —A *Repayer*

Getting donors involved with the nonprofit a step at a time is the key to increasing their personal commitment. Recent findings from the field of relationship development confirm the importance of getting customers to participate in decisions related to their involvement (Crosby and Stephens, 1987; Brown and Swartz, 1989). It has been shown, for example, that people obtaining services are more satisfied if they have been involved, and if they have participated in generating the service itself (File, Judd, and Prince, 1992). That participation is also key to donor satisfaction in working with nonprofits (Cermak, File, and Prince, 1991). On the basis of fund-raiser experience and research, therefore, we would expect that getting donors involved with activities of the non-profit would result in satisfaction. This involvement could be in any number of areas, from involvement in traditional roles such as volunteering and committee work to new ways of participation, all with appropriate reinforcement from the media and from advisors.

Increase Participation to Increase Involvement

From a relationship development perspective, the process of increasing donor participation in the interaction with the nonprofit will be examined. The concept of participation in the interaction goes well beyond a consideration of the traditional roles nonprofits create for donors to play, roles such as fund raiser, board member, charitable recruiter, and the like. Instead, relationship development focuses on increasing the participation of the donor in interactions. Many opportunities are open to fund raisers to increase donor participation, thus fund raisers can facilitate increasing involvement between donor and nonprofit. For example, fund raisers can include obtaining donor input into meeting frequency and agendas, the nature and frequency of information flow, the soliciting of questions and suggestions, and the encouraging of the charity network. As the following sections show, many opportunities to increase donor participation, to build involvement, and to generate long-term loyalty through stronger relationships are available to fund raisers.

Some Donors Would Prefer to Be Asked About
Their Preferences Concerning the Time,
Place, and Frequency of Meetings

Major donors value their time and perceive themselves to
be busy and committed people. Most have been owners of
businesses or senior executives in companies and are used
to people arranging meetings around their schedules and
preferences. In general, these donors perceive that nonprofit
executives do not always ask about their preferences on the
time, place, and frequency of meetings. For these three
aspects of meeting interaction, only some donors recall being asked even occasionally. The exception are Dynasts, who
say they are asked their preferences about meeting frequency
more than half the time. Figure 11.1 shows details.

> They are careful to tell me about upcoming meetings, and I know
> they want me to be there. But I would prefer it if they would
> come right out and ask me what would work best for me.
> —A *Dynast*

> I value all the work this charity is doing, but I notice they have
> their own way of doing things, and I am expected to go along.
> I guess that's how they have to do it, but I would have liked to
> have been asked about the little things, like the time of meet-
> ings, and where they would be.
> —A *Socialite*

In general, it appears that nonprofit executives do not
regularly check with donors about their personal preferences
for meeting times. Members of some philanthropic personalities (Socialites, Altruists, the Devout) cannot recall being
asked sometimes or frequently. Donors are also not generally consulted on where meetings should be held. Donors are
asked somewhat more often about their preferences concerning meeting frequency.

> It's a bit frustrating. I guess I'm used to running the show in my
> own business, to calling the shots. I really know I can't move

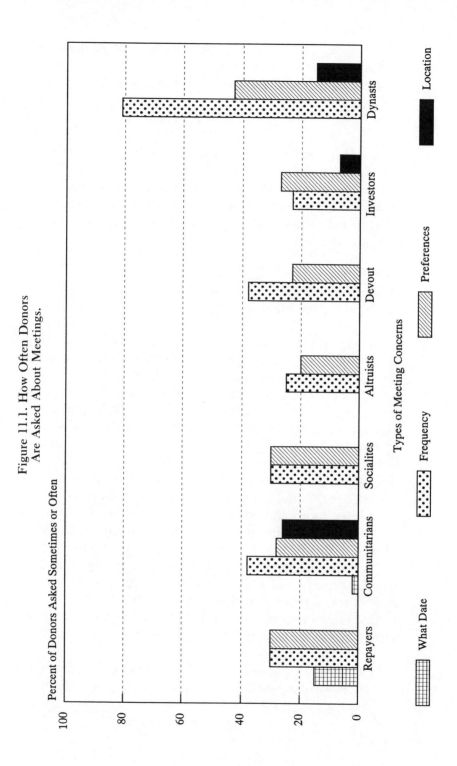

Figure 11.1. How Often Donors
Are Asked About Meetings.

all their meetings around to suit my personal preferences, but it would be nice to be asked.

—A *Communitarian*

I shouldn't complain because of all the good they do, but it seems as though many charities aren't very businesslike. They don't organize meetings well, for example. Unless I am careful, I end up at a meeting where we either wait around and wonder if a key person was ever contacted or where no one really knows why we are together.

—An *Investor*

Donors Would Like to Be Involved in Deciding on Meeting Agendas

Donors would like to be useful, and one way is to be involved in setting the agendas for meetings in which they are involved. However, their experience is that nonprofits do not generally ask them to participate in shaping the agenda for upcoming meetings. As shown in Figure 11.2, fund raisers may have an opportunity to facilitate greater participation by donors. Nonprofits may be missing significant opportunity to increase donor's perceived involvement by not consistently asking them what information they need.

For example, few donors say they are asked even sometimes what topics should be on the agenda at upcoming meetings. Only Communitarians recall to any degree being asked what it is they would like to know about the nonprofit and its operations; in several segments, no one recalled that question being asked of them with any frequency. Few major donors recall being asked for suggestions.

Donors report that nonprofits do, however, generally ask in broad terms about their preferences.

I was asked at the beginning what I'd like to know, and that was great. It would be nice if they ask again, and check in about how I'm doing.

—A *Devout*

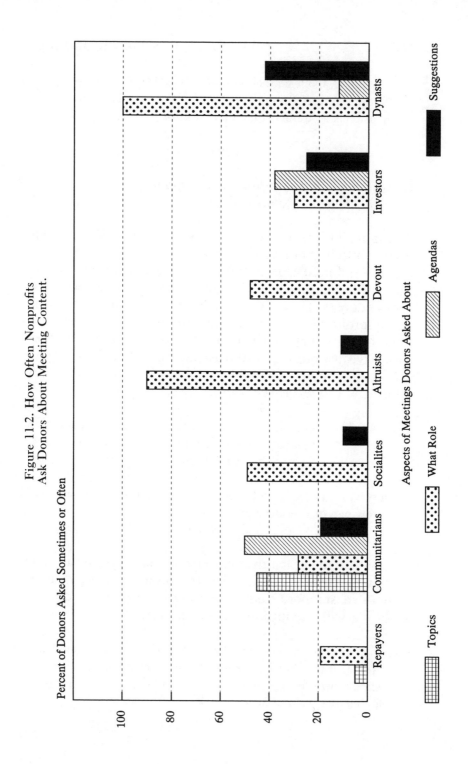

Figure 11.2. How Often Nonprofits
Ask Donors About Meeting Content.

They asked about committees, and did a good job about getting me involved. Recently, I started feeling like I was in a rut,
and it feels as though they don't ask for my suggestions any
more.

—A Repayer

Donors Say That Nonprofits Infrequently Involve Them in Relationships

As Figure 11.3 shows, donors generally say they are rarely
invited into higher levels of involvement. The Figure shows
that five different aspects of interaction are reported as sometimes or frequently occurring by approximately 20 to 60 percent of donors. These five interactions include such behaviors
by nonprofit officers as giving updates on the nonprofit, giving information about the nonprofit, asking donors whether
they have any questions, and asking donors for their suggestions and opinions. Given the modest effort such behaviors
require, these levels seem low.

I really like them at (nonprofit). Andrea calls every few weeks
or so, and always with something I am interested in knowing.

—An Altruist

I just wrote a letter withdrawing my support. I found out about
the change of President in the newspaper.

—A Communitarian

Of all the philanthropic personalities, Dynasts are able
to manage their relationships with nonprofits most successfully. Dynasts more frequently say they are involved in interacting with nonprofits than other types.

I do hear other donors complain about how they are handled
by the charities, but I think it's because they don't make their
wishes known. In my family, we've been taught how to subtly
tell a charity what we need.

—A Dynast

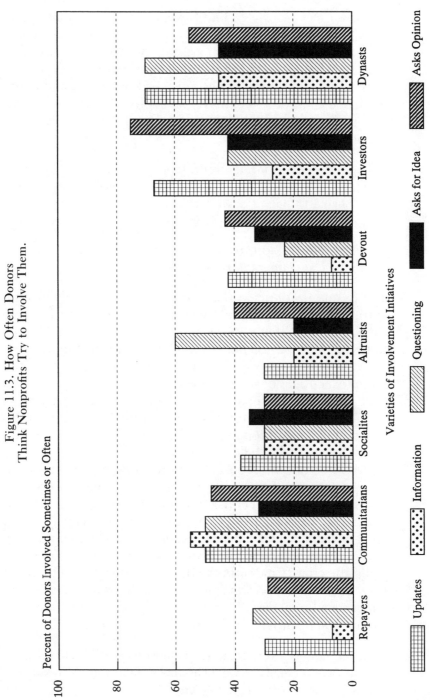

Figure 11.3. How Often Donors
Think Nonprofits Try to Involve Them.

Percent of Donors Involved Sometimes or Often

Varieties of Involvement Intiatives

Updates   Information   Questioning   Asks for Idea   Asks Opinion

By contrast, Repayers are somewhat less likely to feel they have been included in the group getting information from a nonprofit, or in the group asked for advice and counsel. Just a third or less of all Repayers felt that the nonprofit they support most had undertaken any of these involvement actions even occasionally.

> They were all over me during the fund raising phase for the new library. But once they met the goal, it seemed like I never heard the slightest thing for a very long while.
> —A *Repayer*

Donors Believe Nonprofits Do Not Encourage Them to Use Their Charity Networks

The frequency of networking activities varies greatly by philanthropic personality and by type of activity. Overall, however, donors say that nonprofits do not particularly encourage some of the types of networking, as shown in Figure 11.4.

Most donors say they have been introduced to the senior executives of the nonprofit. About 80 percent or more of all types except Repayers and Dynasts feel they have been connected to the officers of the nonprofits they support. So do a slightly lower proportion of Dynasts (62.5%) and a minority of Repayers (42.9%).

Some donors report that nonprofits do refer them to their friends and families for discussion of important topics; this seems to happen consistently to Altruists (100.0%), and frequently to Socialites (95.6%), Communitarians (75.4%), and Dynasts (75.1%). This shows some evidence that the nonprofits these donors are affiliated with are working on leveraging the charity networks of the philanthropists. Far fewer Devout (43.6%), Investors (40.6%), and Repayers (38.1%) are encouraged to access their personal networks for their own support or to provide referrals to the nonprofit.

> Robert has been very comfortable to work with. Whenever he brings a new project he would like my support with, he tells me to talk it over with my family first.
> —An *Altruist*

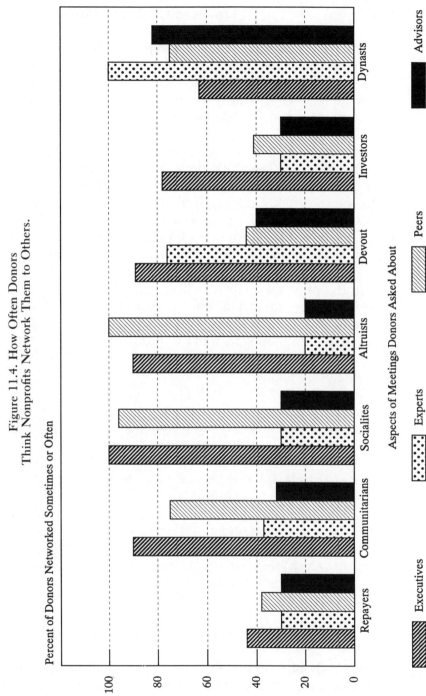

Figure 11.4. How Often Donors
Think Nonprofits Network Them to Others.

Percent of Donors Networked Sometimes or Often

Aspects of Meetings Donors Asked About

Executives

Experts

Peers

Advisors

> One of the things I have liked about (nonprofit) is that they keep
> urging me to talk everything over with my accountant and law-
> yer. They have even suggested we all get together a couple of
> times to be sure the thing is structured right.
>   —An Investor

Referral of major donors to advisors or including financial experts is less frequently done. Except for Dynasts, less
than 40 percent of each philanthropic personality said they
had been referred to a legal or financial advisor in connection with a giving process. Except for the Devout and Dynasts, less than 40 percent of each philanthropic personality
said they had been introduced to financial experts through
the offices of the nonprofit. This finding is consistent with
that in the previous chapter, where a gap is shown to exist
between donor interest in the more sophisticated giving
strategies and the frequency with which nonprofits suggest
these strategies. It appears that nonprofits are not accessing
the financial networks and advisory networks on behalf of
their major donors.

> I am interested in giving, but I am also interested in avoiding
> the tax man. Everything was fine when I was giving smaller gifts,
> but when I wanted to structure something a little more compli-
> cated, the charity seemed to fall apart. They didn't know what
> they were doing, and it cooled me on the whole deal.
>   —An Investor

> It always seems as though I have to bring in the new ideas on
> financial giving to them through my husband. He's a financial
> analyst, so he knows what you can do these days, but he's get-
> ting tired of always being the one.
>   —A Socialite

Increasing Involvement Increases Commitment

A large body of evidence in development, and services development, confirms the importance of involvement in un-

derstanding behavior (Greenwald and Leavitt, 1985; Day, 1970). As the feeling of involvement increases through an increase in participation, commitment to the product or service follows (Clarke and Belk, 1979; Zaichkowsky, 1985), as does interest in discussing it with others (Richins and Root-Shaffer, 1988), and so does consumption. Translated into nonprofit terms, we would expect to see positive relationships between donors' feelings of involvement and their intention to increase support, their intention to become more involved in volunteering, their willingness to raise funds from others, and their willingness to encourage others to become more personally involved. All these flow from feelings of higher involvement produced by participation.

Conceptually, generating involvement through increased participation is the act of empowerment. When a philanthropist is empowered, he or she is given power—a feeling, a belief, a sense of control. Donor empowerment does not imply that the officers of the nonprofit forsake their fiduciary responsibilities. To the contrary, from an operational perspective, the control of the nonprofit remains steadfastly in the hands of its officers. Empowering a philanthropist should be understood in terms of generating involvement and participation. Making the major donor feel an integral part of the functioning of the nonprofit is critical to the success of long-term relationship management.

More Intense Feelings of Involvement Are Associated with the Intention to Give More

Service firms increasingly recognize the importance of current customers in a comprehensive program of revenue generation. In general, securing additional transactions from current customers requires less investment than identifying and developing new customers (Maister, 1989; Crane, 1989). However, current customers must be well served and satisfied to be interested in new transactions.

In this context, it is noteworthy that the various philanthropic personality groups display wide variation in whether they plan to increase their support. Altruists, Dynasts, Repayers, and the Devout are the most likely to say they will increase giving (90.0%, 81.3%, 81.0%, and 77.7%, respectively).

> I give as a long term commitment, even if it looks as though results don't show up right away.
> — A *Repayer*

> Supporting charities is not like buying shoes. It's important to stay with them year in and year out, and not change around each season.
> — A *Dynast*

By contrast, most Socialites, Communitarians, and Investors do not plan to increase their giving (only 29.8%, 26.1%, and 21.9% respectively say they do). These groups are the most attuned to changes in the local scene and to a group sense of what is appropriate to support at any given time. These groups are more responsive to changes in condition and thinking.

> We like to support a few charities for a time and help them get on their feet, and then move on to a new group.
> — A *Socialite*

Across all groups, however, the higher the sense of donor involvement, the more likely they are to plan to increase donations (correlation coefficient of .6483, highly significant $p < .001$). Involvement significantly affects the future propensity of major donors to increase their level of support.

The Higher the Involvement, the More Some Philanthropists Plan to Volunteer

Overall, most major donors do not plan to become more personally involved in volunteer activities on behalf of nonprofits. More of the Devout do (33.3%) than any other segment, for example Investors (15.6%), Socialites (13.0%), Dynasts (12.5%), Repayers (9.5%), and Communitarians (5.3%).

It's not like I wouldn't want to do more volunteering, but there just isn't time.
— *An Altruist*

Major donors do understand that their perceived primary value to the nonprofit sector is as philanthropists rather than as volunteers. Volunteering is concentrated in philanthropic personalities for whom it has a specific payoff — charity events for Socialites, board room networking for Communitarians, selfless service by the Devout.

However, an intention to volunteer at any level is once again significantly associated with involvement (correlation coefficient .6119, highly significant at $p < .001$). As involvement increases, so does the willingness to personally volunteer, although the levels of volunteering are generally lower than the levels for giving financial support.

The More the Involvement, the Greater the Willingness to Recommend the Nonprofit to Others

The higher the feelings of involvement, the more major donors are inclined to recommend to others that they, too, support the nonprofit with cash gifts and voluntary activity. The relationship between involvement and the propensity to encourage peers to donate is high (correlation of .4402) and significant ($p < .001$), as is the relationship between involvement and the propensity to encourage peers to volunteer (correlation of .4087, $p < .001$). Thus, involvement impels major donors to speak well of the nonprofit as they move through their charity networks, and to join in the effort to develop new donors.

It's part of my life. I'm usually doing something for or about (the charity) every day, so it's natural that I encourage other friends I know to buy a table or make a small gift.
— *A Socialite*

You have to understand, I am in meetings with and about charities several times a week. Sure, the ones I talk about are the

ones I'm most involved with, the ones that seem to have something going on.
                                        —A *Communitarian*

Donor Commitment Is Reinforced Through Promotion and Intermediaries

Once a relationship has been established between donor and
nonprofit, and once the participation and involvement building blocks of relationship development have been put in
place, then the nonprofit can develop ways to augment that
interpersonal relationship. This reinforcement can occur in
two general areas. One is through media relations such as
newsletters and public relations. The other is through professional advisors who are part of the charity network. These
mechanisms to reinforce major donor commitment are discussed below. It should be noted that because all these channels of influence are less personal, they are no substitute for
direct, one-on-one relationship development efforts.

Although Newsletters or Magazines from Nonprofits Have Little Impact on a Wealthy Philanthropist's Decision to Become Involved with a Nonprofit, They Have a Role in Later Relationship-Sustaining Activities

As could be expected, few (0.9%) major donors identify newsletters or magazines as being very important in their decision to become involved with a nonprofit.

> There is nothing a newsletter is going to tell me that will make
> me interested in a nonprofit group. Blowing your own whistle
> is not going to make me want to become interested in them.
>   —A *Devout*

> Everybody sends us junk mail. And, I get all kinds of magazines
> and papers from plenty of charities. Once in a while I might send
> one of them a check for a few dollars, but I'm not going to do
> much more just because of a magazine.
>   —A *Socialite*

However, publications sent by a nonprofit can be a way of increasing donor involvement in later stages of relationship building. While they cannot replace person-to-person interaction, they can reinforce involvement already created by a relationship development program. Recent technological advances make it possible to create versions of media such as newsletters for each different segment of readers.

> I do like the mailings from (the charity). I know what's going on, but I like to see what they are telling others.
> — A Communitarian

> You know, I spend so much money with (nonprofit), that I actually like those little newsletters. Seeing all their activities reminds me it is a good cause.
> — An Altruist

Care should be taken, however, that the tone and execution of publications generated by the nonprofit are both in keeping with its mission and appropriate for the expectations of its major donors. Perceived overspending on publications can backfire, for example, if a nonprofit numbers many Investors in its base of donors.

> They can put out the fanciest publication and that's not going to impress me. It's not going to get me to get committed to them. It would turn me off. I'd rather see them put the money into doing what they're about, helping the homeless, fixing the environment, or whatever it is, they have to have better things to do with the money people give them than put out fancy booklets and papers.
> — An Investor

Public Relations Pieces Stimulate Interest and Reinforce Relationships, Particularly Among Community-Minded Donors

Anecdotal evidence shows that the use of public relations can be quite effective in soliciting smaller donations and may even draw the attention of wealthy donors. Nonetheless, public relations in and of itself will not prove a particularly viable means of attracting wealthy philanthropists to become heavily involved in a nonprofit. It is simply not compelling enough. As shown, donors are attracted to nonprofits through the interpersonal relationships of their charity network. The affluent prefer to stay within their peer groups.

> If I read about something that pulls at my heart strings, I'd send a check, maybe a pretty big check if it's a real strong pull at my heart strings. But, that's a one time thing. My true responsibility is to the charities I'm involved with, and a story no matter how sad is not what gets me to be involved.
> —A *Socialite*

> There will always be sad songs and the media will always dramatize them. That doesn't mean we all have to run out and do something about them. It'll be like putting out the small brush fires. I want to put out the inferno. So, I'm not swayed by stories, no matter how sad. I decided to join and support the Church's youth services programs so the brush fires do not become the big fires.
> —A *Devout*

Major donors do welcome public relations about a nonprofit they support in a significant way, as it reinforces and validates their commitment. Socialites, Communitarians, and the Devout, with their community orientation, especially respond favorably to public relations. Investors believe public relations reflects well on their choice, and Repayers appreciate the greater visibility given the cause they back. Dynasts and Altruists are more ambivalent, but not opposed.

> Sure it makes me feel good, proud even, that a program we got off the ground gets a great write-up in the paper. People helping people is what will turn this community around.
> —A *Communitarian*

I liked seeing the big play in the local news about the new hospital clinic opening. It reminded me how good I feel to have helped
make treatment a little more available for kids.

—A Repayer

Advisors to the Affluent Can Reinforce Relationships Between Donors and Nonprofits

As seen, advisors to the affluent are important members of
the charity network, and influential in the early stages of
the relationship between an increasing number of donors
and the nonprofits they support. Once the donor-nonprofit
relationship has developed, however, the role of this advisor
does not diminish, but may become more prominent as the
donor evolves from simple current giving to more complex
planned giving strategies. Resource development executives need to target these advisors as influencers in major
giving and, not incidentally, as prospective donors in their
own right.

When I could finally afford to be generous like I always wanted
to be, Carl, my accountant, proved to be a big help. He introduced me around, taught me that giving was damn hard—if
I wanted to do it right, and I did. His recommendations about
who to give to carried a lot of weight with me. Many years and
a lot of giving later, they still do.

—A Communitarian

I know my business. I can feel the health of the business like
I know how my own body feels. For charity, I need help. I have
these advisors and I get them to open the doors for me, have
them make introductions and I still use them as a sounding board
whenever anything big comes up.

—An Investor

McArthur has been a confidant of the family as long as I can
remember. When I came into my money (trust fund) I went to
him and he helped me determine who's out there. I check with

him on charity related decisions. He taught me what it means
to be a [name of family].
— A *Dynast*

Because of the importance of advisors to the affluent,
fund raisers should apply the same strategies to cultivate them
as they should use with philanthropists. When working with
the advisor of a nonprofit, fund raisers should reinforce the
vision of the nonprofit that is important to the advisor's client
(the nonprofit's donor). All the participation- and involvement-
inducing strategies of relationship development should be
used with these advisors. Over time, the systematic application of relationship development programs to advisors will
result in an extensive network. This network of intermediaries in turn can produce wealthy donor referrals (as described
in Chapter Eight). Substantial relationships with advisors can
only result in reinforced relationships with philanthropists.

When I was first considering a trust, I was worried because it
seemed so complicated. There were many ways it could go
wrong. But it turned out that the fund raiser knew my accountant, and she helped him make a good connection to my attorney, so the whole thing came off well.
— An *Investor*

My advisor has waved me off a few charities I was considering.
He had bad dealings with them in the past.
— A *Dynast*

Moreover, the use of philanthropic advisors is a growing trend. Nonprofits should respond to this new development in philanthropy by positioning themselves effectively
with respect to these advisors. By being able to develop strong
relationships with advisors, the nonprofit can concurrently
develop strong relationships with philanthropists.

Implications

To empower donors, a nonprofit has to create strategies for
meaningful participation by donors that stimulate positive

feelings of involvement. Involvement and participation generate the kind of donor commitment that results in financial support, volunteer support, and charitable recruiting on behalf of the nonprofit. Indirect means of reinforcement—such as promotion and relationships with advisors—are also critical in the relationship development mix.

The personal touch possible through the participation and involvement aspects of relationship development is required with the financially advantaged. Relationship development begins through the process of referrals. That is, a trusted intermediary introduces the nonprofit to the philanthropist-prospect. Because of that trust, the wealthy are willing to take the time and make the effort to consider the charitable organization. At this point, the challenge is to communicate value in the terms most appropriate to the individual philanthropic personality. As we have seen, this is accomplished through crafting a vision which reflects the donors' philanthropic motivations. Then, the appropriate giving strategies need to be brought forward. Finally, a program of relationship development must be established to build long-lasting involvement and participation.

Participation Is the Key to Empowerment and Involvement

- Work interactively with philanthropists on logistical matters.

    Encourage philanthropists to provide input on the administrative aspects of meetings. Encourage them to state their preferences as to when and how often to meet. In effect, let them indicate the level of contact they are most comfortable with.

    Similarly, encourage donors to suggest where these meetings should take place. The goal is to make them comfortable.

    Though the issues are minor, fund raisers empower the philanthropists by seeking their opinions and thereby strengthen the bond between major donor and nonprofit.

- Work with philanthropists on deciding the content of interactions.

    Encourage the philanthropist to react to suggested discussion topics of the meetings whenever possible. These topics will concern the nonprofit and this process demonstrates the regard the organization has for the philanthropist.

    Solicit information concerning what major donors want to know about the nonprofit. Asking questions can enable the nonprofit to quell any anxieties and eliminate any doubts.

    Ensure that philanthropists are provided with meeting agendas. This communicates a high degree of organization as well as respect for the importance of time to these affluent individuals.

- Engage philanthropists on the nature of the relationship.

    Provide frequent and focused updates on the nonprofit. Also, provide information concerning the mission and vision of the nonprofit. The focus of updates and background information should be slanted to the interests of that philanthropic personality.

    Actively solicit questions, suggestions, and opinions from major donors. In this way, fund raisers directly empower major donors. In a relationship development context, all questions must be rapidly and adequately answered and all suggestions must be seriously considered. If a suggestion is implemented, the fact must be brought to the attention of the philanthropist. More importantly, if a suggestion is not implemented, then a clearly articulated reason for not doing so must be provided to the philanthropist.

- Promote philanthropists to use their charity networks.

    Ensure that major donors have the opportunity to interact with the people running the nonprofit. Senior officers need to take the time to communicate that the trust given to them by the philanthropist is earned. Many major donors do not want to get involved in the day-to-day running of the nonprofit, yet they want the reassurance that these individuals are competent.

Encourage philanthropists to discuss their experiences with the nonprofit with friends, family, and business associates. This will prove particularly advantageous as it promotes the leveraging of the charity networks that is so essential in attracting new philanthropists to the nonprofit (see the Introduction).

Selectively introduce major donors to advisors, especially financial experts. The object here is to set the stage for the development of planned gifts. As seen in the previous chapter, major donors have a significant interest in private foundations as well as charitable remainder trusts. For most nonprofits, to effectively promote this giving strategy requires certain legal and financial expertise that may not be present in-house. Therefore, strategic alliances are recommended. In addition, this is also a way of subsequently attracting prospective major donors.

Empower Philanthropists Through Involvement

- Empowering major donors is achieved by generating involvement.

    Involvement is a psychological construct well established in development.

    Feelings of increased involvement on the part of the donor result in the desire to give more, volunteer more, and engage in greater amounts of charitable recruiting.

Strengthen the Relationship Through Promotion and Intermediaries

- Employ print media to create an ongoing dialogue with major donors.

    Newsletters or magazines will create a constant communication channel with major donors.

The content of print communications must reinforce the belief among major donors that their decision to support the nonprofit is a wise one. This requires understanding the philanthropic personalities of the recipients of these communications and providing specific messages to each.

- Use public relations to raise the perceived value of the nonprofit.

  If the nonprofit is deemed newsworthy for positive reasons, then major donors, particularly those who are community-minded, feel that their support of the organization is indeed confirmed.

  Develop relationships with local media as they are always interested in promoting nonprofits. It is a win-win for all.

- Apply relationship development strategies with advisors to the affluent.

  Advisors must be seen as allies. Therefore, it is critical to cultivate them in the same manner philanthropists are cultivated. The same approaches will be effective with these individuals as they are with major donors.

  Doing so will provide cost-effective technical expertise as well as the opportunity to be introduced to wealthy prospects.

Conclusion:

Applying the Seven Faces Framework

The previous chapters have outlined a four-step process development officers can add to their fund-raising programs designed to obtain support from affluent individual donors. There is, however, another opportunity for applying the Seven Faces framework that can be initiated immediately. We present this opportunity in the form of a self-rating checklist to enable fund raisers to move from the book and an understanding of the Seven Faces framework to personal experience applying the model.

The opportunity is to communicate to current major donors how much they are valued, and to communicate with them using the insights of the Seven Faces framework. The immediate opportunity for nonprofits lies in the finding that donors can feel undervalued by nonprofits. Relatively few donors say that the nonprofits they interact with most seem to value them as highly as they think they should be valued in some areas. This is where the value gap appears. (See Figure C.1.) While it has become axiomatic in nonprofit circles to recognize and thank donors—"thank a donor seven times"—it is revealing that these major donors generally do not feel as valued as they think they could be. They appreci-

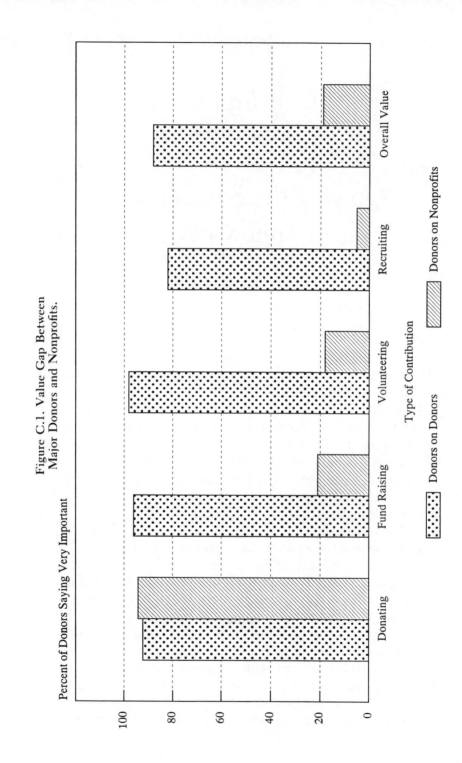

Figure C.1. Value Gap Between
Major Donors and Nonprofits.

ate the thanks they do get, but want participation as well in order to feel valued.

Question 1: How Has Your Nonprofit Expressed Appreciation to Affluent Individual Donors for Their Fund-raising Efforts?

In the area of fund raising, philanthropists generally feel they are highly effective in soliciting contributions from others, but they also feel that nonprofits would rate them low in terms of development support. Socialites and Communitarians are the two philanthropic styles most active in fund raising, and both welcome recognition given in such a way that it is seen by their peer groups. Repayers are active at behind-the-scenes fund raising, best at one-on-one contacts with people who share their relationship with the nonprofit. Most Repayers, however, do not want public honors, but tangible demonstrations that their support has helped the constituents with whom they identify. Investors are gratified when management and financial reports are shared with them. The Devout feel valued when their efforts are acknowledged using the concepts and language of their religious tradition. Altruists need their philanthropic values mirrored back to them.

Question 2: How Has Your Nonprofit Shown Affluent Individual Donors That Their Volunteer Activity Is Valued?

The wealthy rate their volunteer activities very highly. In many cases, they provide to nonprofits for free what they can command considerable value for commercially in terms of business and management expertise. In other cases, the affluent have an elevated sense of the value of their own time, and expect nonprofits to value it as they do. By and large, the wealthy feel they are not as valued as they could be by nonprofits.

As shown earlier, the key to involving affluent individual

donors is to increase their participation. Joint planning of meetings, down to such decisions as time, place, and agenda, builds participation and increases feelings of being involved and being valued. However, these donors want to volunteer in very different arenas — a donor who is mismatched with an area of volunteer activity will feel as though he or she is not contributing optimally. Repayers, Altruists, and to a lesser extent Dynasts prefer to volunteer in support of constituent activities. Investors will gravitate toward finance committees, while Communitarians are most comfortable as trustees or members of planning committees. Socialites resist becoming involved in activities other than fund-raising events. The Seven Faces framework can provide nonprofits with another check on whether the volunteer activities of affluent individual donors are optimally focused.

Question 3: How Does Your Nonprofit Show Affluent Individual Donors That Their Recruiting of Other Volunteers Is Valued?

This is another area where a significant gap exists in perceptions. Affluent individual donors feel they are a valuable asset in that they can enlist other wealthy people to become involved with a nonprofit as volunteers. However, they do not feel that nonprofits value them for this role as highly as they could. Communitarians are more likely to recruit other business owners for nonprofits who help them develop and nurture informal relationships with other community leaders which in turn can help them in their business roles. Socialites appreciate when others understand the group nature and the complexities of their social network, and when nonprofits help them, in turn, "take care" of that network.

Question 4: How Does Your Nonprofit Show Affluent Individual Donors That Their Personal Donations Are Valued?

In only one area, personal donations, do philanthropists feel that their contribution is important and also feel that nonprofits think their contribution is important. There is no gap here; philanthropists feel appreciated. Almost all (96.2%) feel their financial support to the nonprofit sector is important, and almost all believe nonprofits are fulsome in their appreciation and thanks. Each of the Seven Faces feels valued for current giving; the opportunity lies in helping donors feel equally valued for their other forms of support.

Summary

The Seven Faces framework is a model for understanding the motivations of affluent individual donors. Its strength and appeal lie in its apparent simplicity and broad applicability to development situations. Its limitation also lies in its simplicity. There are no easy answers to how to attract and cultivate the affluent. It requires rigorous and demanding day-in-and-day-out work on relationship development. Because the Seven Faces approach is a model, it will not, of course, exactly fit every donor, nor every nonprofit, nor every situation. Our experience in actual relationship development situations shows that the most effective fund raisers add the Seven Faces model to their own expertise as another perspective for understanding donors, rather than as a replacement for prior knowledge. In working with the expert fund raisers who helped develop and test the framework, it has become clear that the implementation of the Seven Faces of philanthropy principles does help bring it to life and produce success.

By understanding why different affluent and charitable individuals give — their philanthropic personalities — a fund raiser can first identify the particular charity networks potential wealthy donors belong to. Knowledge of these charity networks is the first step in the donor-cultivation process. Initial approaches to a prospective donor are general, then increasingly tailored to the philanthropic personality as it becomes known. With this knowledge, fund raisers can craft a vision which will meaningfully link the mission of the nonprofit to the benefits sought by a donor of a specific philanthropic personality. The fund raiser can then promote appropriate charitable giving strategies and empower the wealthy prospect. This process transforms the wealthy prospect into a wealthy donor — a philanthropist.

Appendix:
Research Methodology

Methods familiar to the social sciences for insuring reliability and validity of the results were used in the studies on which this book is based. A description of the methodologies used in the principal study is provided here.

Sampling

Because of the low incidence of major donors and their personal concern for privacy, the customary social science methods of random sampling from a known population cannot be used. For example, a major recent national survey on giving had, as the top income category, all those who earned $100,000 and over and contributed an average of $2,329 — a group whose economic status is well below the major donors of interest here and in other studies of this elite population (Hodgkinson, Weitzman, and the Gallup Organization, 1988). Clearly, identifying and interviewing the very affluent involves tradeoffs — either systematic sampling procedures need to be set aside in favor of networking to obtain interviews (Schervish, 1988; Odendahl, 1991) or systematic sampling techniques can be used if there is a willingness to accept data provided by associates or employees of the donor rather than the donor personally (Boris, 1987). This study employed a specific form of the networking approach, called snowball sampling, which is akin to cluster sampling. Snowball sampling carries with it the attendant risks of being unable to reliably project to the population under study.

Where the population of interest is severely limited and difficult to identify, snowball (Biernacki and Waldorf, 1981) or multiplicity (Rothbart and others, 1982) sampling methods are employed. In these methods, members of special populations are located by referral. The advantage is cost-effective identification of respondents; the disadvantage is the inability to estimate sampling error. These methods are useful, however, in creating perspective on the research questions (Churchill, 1991).

Since the sampling objective was to create a sample of affluent persons making major contributions to nonprofits, a two-phase snowball sample was created. In the first phase, the design attempted to compensate for the homogeneity of social networks by networking through a number of professional service firms with an affluent clientele (such as the private banking divisions of major investment houses and major law firms), by creating a number of clustering centers, and by collecting as large a sample as possible. Ultimately, twelve professional service firms from across the United States were enlisted. Because of institutional interest in the topic of financial planning among the affluent, these firms agreed to participate. These firms received a summary of the research results in return for their participation in the study. In the second phase of sampling, participating institutions identified 218 affluent clients meeting the study criteria.

Questionnaire

The questionnaire contained an extensive battery of motivational items drawn from the literature (refer to the Introduction for a discussion of previous studies). It also covered aspects of charity network participation before and after the choice of a specific nonprofit to support. The charity network batteries reflected the aspects of valence, direction, and voice—subsets of word-of-mouth for some time (Hirschman, 1970). In addition, extensive data was collected on the types of nonprofits supported, the magnitude of giving in recent years and attitudes of the affluent as to how they were viewed by nonprofits. Finally, family, economic, and other background data were collected.

Analysis

As suggested by Hair, Anderson, Tatham, and Black (1992) the sample was randomly split into a sample for analysis and a hold-out sample. Using the analytic sample, cluster analysis was conducted on the items in the motivational battery. Unlike factor analysis (which groups similar attitudes, the approach selected by Boris, 1987), cluster analysis groups people based on the similarity of their attitudes. Hierarchical cluster analysis based on nearest centroid sorting was selected for this study because it is consistent with statistical methods for benefit segmentation and because the outcome—groups of people—is intuitively easier to grasp. Inspection of the dendrogram plots enabled us to establish the pattern of outliers and observe the cluster structure. Following Hair and others (1992) we considered several solutions and the results of both data sets before settling on the seven-group solution; visual inspection of the dendrograms revealed a jump in what are variously called amalgamation or fusion coefficients (Churchill, 1991) or error variability measures (Hair and others, 1992) at that point. In addition, the population in each cluster was better balanced than in other solutions, and the item structure shaping each cluster provided the greatest descriptive appeal. The original and hold-out samples were then combined for reporting here. Descriptive statistics for these clusters were calculated on the remaining variables (not used in the clustering) to generate a data-based profile for each philanthropic market segment.

Validation

To validate the results, two complementary approaches were taken. In the first approach, the cluster solution—the philanthropic personality framework—was tested and discussed with two focus groups of nonprofit resource development managers and heads of nonprofits who confirmed its relevance and validity in the context of their own experience. The second approach to an exploration of validity was reinterviewing the respondents. One of the authors recontacted members of each segment and interviewed them at length over the telephone about their motivations for giving. These follow-up interviews validated donors' segment membership as determined statistically in all cases. Direct quotes of respondents from these follow-up interviews are included in the segment profiles and in the section on relationship development.

Follow-up Studies

Over the course of these validation interviews, it was found that certain language was effective in discussing philanthropy with one segment or another. Lists of images words were compiled across the set of interviews, and the entire major donor sample was resurveyed. This time, major donors were given the list of images and asked to use a 10-point scale to indicate how important each word was to them and their motives for giving personally. Results of this follow-up survey are provided in Chapter Eleven.

References

AAFRC Trust for Philanthropy. *Giving USA*. New York: AAFRC Trust for Philanthropy, 1989.

Ben-Ner, A., and Van Hoomissen, T. "The Growth of the Nonprofit Sector in the 1980s: Facts and Interpretation." *Nonprofit Management and Leadership*, 1990, 1(2), 99–116.

Biernacki, P., and Waldorf, D. "Snowball Sampling: Problems and Techniques of Chair Referred Sampling." *Sociological Methods and Research*, 1981, 10, 141–163.

Boris, E. "Creation and Growth: A Survey of Private Foundations." In T. Odendahl (ed.), *American's Wealthy and the Future of Foundations*. New York: Foundation Center, 1987.

Brown, S. W., and Swartz, T. A. "A Gap Analysis of Professional Service Quality." *Journal of Marketing*, 1989, 53, 92–98.

Cermak, D.S.P., File, K. M., and Prince, R. A. "Complaining and Praising in Non-Profit Exchanges: When Satisfaction Matters Less." *Journal of Consumer Satisfaction, Dissatisfaction, and Complaining Behavior*, 1991, 4, 180–187.

Cermak, D.S.P., File, K. M., and Prince, R. A. "A Benefit Segmentation of the Major Donor Market." *Journal of Business Research*, 1994, 29(2), 121–130.

Churchill, G. A. *Marketing Research: Methodological Founda-tions.* Chicago: Dryden Press, 1991.

Cialdini, R. B. *Influence.* New York: Quill, 1984.

Clarke, K., and Belk, R. W. "The Effects of Product Involve-ment and Task Definition on Anticipated Consumer Effort." In *Advances in Consumer Research.* Vol. 6. Ann Arbor, Mich.: Association for Consumer Research, 1979.

Congram, C. A., and Dumesic, R. J. *The Accountant's Stra-tegic Marketing Guide.* New York: Wiley, 1986.

Crane, F. G. "A Practical Guide to Professional Services Mar-keting." *Journal of Professional Services Marketing,* 1989, 5(1), 3–15.

Crosby, L. A., and Stephens, N. "The Effects of Relation-ship Marketing on Satisfaction, Retention, and Prices in the Life Insurance Industry." *Journal of Marketing Research,* 1987, 24, 404–411.

Day, G. S. *Buyer Attitudes and Brand Choice.* New York: Free Press, 1970.

Ensman, R., Jr. "Ten Predictions for the Next Decade." *Fund Raising Management,* 1992, 23(5), 54–55, 60.

Ferguson, J. M., and Brown, S. W. "Relationship Marketing and Association Management." *Journal of Professional Ser-vices Marketing,* 1991, 7(2), 137–147.

Festinger, L. *A Theory of Cognitive Dissonance.* Stanford, Calif.: Stanford University Press, 1957.

File, K. M., Judd, B. B., and Prince, R. A. "The Influence of Participation on Positive Word-of-Mouth and Referrals." *Journal of Services Marketing,* 1992, 6(4), 5–14.

File, K. M., and Prince, R. A. "Positive Word-of-Mouth: Cus-tomer Satisfaction and Buyer Behavior." *International Jour-nal of Bank Marketing,* 1992, 10(1), 25–29.

George, W. R. "Internal Marketing and Organizational Be-havior: A Partnership in Developing Customer-Conscious Employees at Every Level." *Journal of Business Research,* 1990, 20(1), 63–70.

Greenwald, A. G., and Leavitt, C. "Cognitive Theory and Au-dience Involvement." In L. Alwitt and A. Mitchell (eds.), *Psychological Processes and Advertising Effects.* Hillsdale, N.J.: Erlbaum, 1985.

Gronroos, C. "Relationship Approach to Marketing in Service Contexts: The Marketing and Organizational Behavior Interface." *Journal of Business Research*, 1990, 20(1), 3–11.

Guy, B. S., and Patton, W. E. "The Marketing of Altruistic Causes: Understanding Why People Help." *Journal of Services Marketing*, 1988, 2, 5–16.

Hair, J. F., Anderson, R. E., Tatham, R. L., and Black, W. C. *Multivariate Data Analysis*. New York: Macmillan, 1992.

Harvey, J. W. "Benefit Segmentation for Fund Raisers." *Journal of the Academy of Marketing Science*, 1990, 18(1), 77–86.

Herr, P. M., Kordes, F. R., and Kim, J. "Effects of Word-of-Mouth and Product Attribute Information on Persuasion: An Accessibility and Diagnosticity Perspective." *Journal of Consumer Research*, 1991, 17, 454–462.

Hirschman, A. O. *Exit, Voice, and Loyalty: Responses to a Decline in Firms, Organizations, and States*. Cambridge, Mass.: Harvard University Press, 1970.

Hodgkinson, V., Weitzman, M., and the Gallup Organization. *Giving and Volunteering in the United States: 1988 Edition*. Washington, D.C.: Independent Sector, 1988.

Illingworth, J. D. "Relationship Marketing: Pursuing the Perfect Person-to-Person Relationship." *Journal of Services Marketing*, 1991, 5(4), 49–52.

Jencks, C. "Who Gives to What?" In W. W. Powell (ed.), *The Nonprofit Sector: A Research Handbook*. New Haven, Conn.: Yale University Press, 1987.

Johnson, E. M. "Marketing Planning for Nonprofit Organizations." *Nonprofit World*, 1986, 4, 20–21, 38.

Kotler, P. *Marketing Management* (7th ed.) Englewood Cliffs, N.J.: Prentice Hall, 1991.

Leibtag, B. "Marketing to the Affluent." *Journal of Accountancy*, 1986, 162(2), 65–71.

McMurtry, S. L., Netting, F. E., and Kettner, P. M. "How Nonprofits Adapt to a Stringent Environment." *Nonprofit Management and Leadership*, 1991, 1(3), 235–252.

Magat, R. *Prospective Views of Research on Philanthropy and the Voluntary Sector*. New York: Foundation Center, 1990.

Maister, D. H. "Marketing to Existing Clients." *Journal of Management Consulting*, 1989, 5(2), 25–32.

Morgan, R. E., and Chadha, S. "Relationship Marketing at the Service Encounter: The Case of Life Insurance." *Service Industries Journal,* 1993, *13*(1), 112–125.

Odendahl, T. *Charity Begins at Home: Generosity and Self-Interest Among the Philanthropic Elite.* New York: Basic Books, 1990.

Ostrander, S. A., and Schervish, P. G. "Giving and Getting: Philanthropy as Social Relation." In J. Van Til and Associates, *Critical Issues in American Philanthropy: Strengthening Theory and Practice.* San Francisco: Jossey-Bass, 1990.

Panus, J. *Megagifts: Who Gives Them, Who Gets Them.* Chicago: Pluribus Press, 1984.

Plummer, J. T. "The Concept and Application of Life Style Segmentation." *Journal of Marketing,* 1974, *38*, 33–37.

Prince, R. A. *Marketing Investment Management Services: The Art and Science of Creating and Keeping Investors.* Dublin, Ireland: Lafferty Publications, 1991.

Prince, R. A., File, K. M., and Gillespie, J. "Philanthropic Styles." *Nonprofit Management and Leadership,* 1993, *3*(3), 255–268.

Reingen, P. H., and Kernan, J. B. "Analysis of Referral Networks in Marketing: Methods and Illustration." *Journal of Marketing Research,* 1986, *23*, 370–379.

Richins, M. L. "Word-of-Mouth by Dissatisfied Consumers: A Pilot Study." *Journal of Marketing,* 1983, *47*, 58–78.

Richins, M. L., and Root-Shaffer, T. "The Role of Involvement and Opinion Leadership in Consumer Word-of-Mouth: An Implicit Model Made Explicit," In *Advances in Consumer Research.* Vol. 15. Ann Arbor, Mich.: Association for Consumer Research, 1988.

Rothbart, G. S., Fine, M., and Sudman, S. "On Finding and Interviewing Needles in the Haystack: The Use of Multiplicity Sampling." *Public Opinion Quarterly,* 1982, *46*, 408–421.

Schervish, P. G. "Philanthropy Among the Wealthy: Empowerment, Motivation, and Strategy." Paper presented to the Rocky Mountain Philanthropic Institute, Vail, Colo. July 1991.

Schervish, P. G., and Herman, A. *Final Report: The Study on Wealth and Philanthropy*. Boston: Social Welfare Research Institute, Boston College, 1988.

Seymour, H. *Designs for Fund Raising*. New York: McGraw-Hill, 1966.

Smith, S. M. "Giving to Charitable Organizations: A Behavioral Review and Framework for Increasing Commitment." In *Advances in Consumer Research*. Vol. 17. Ann Arbor, Mich.: Association for Consumer Research, 1990.

Weisbrod, B. A. *The Nonprofit Economy*. Cambridge, Mass.: Harvard University Press, 1988.

Wills, G. "Dividing and Conquering: Strategies for Segmentation." *International Journal of Bank Marketing*, 1985, 3, 36–46.

Wind, Y. "Issues and Advances in Segmentation Research." *Journal of Marketing Research*, 1978, 15, 317–337.

Wuthnow, R., Hodgkinson, V. A., and Associates. *Faith and Philanthropy in America: Exploring the Role of Religion in America's Voluntary Sector*. San Francisco: Jossey-Bass, 1990.

Zaichkowsky, J. L. "Familiarity: Product Use, Involvement, or Expertise?" In *Advances in Consumer Research*. Vol. 12. Ann Arbor, Mich.: Association for Consumer Research, 1985.

Index